SIGHT WORDS

WORKBOOK

Primer

This book belongs to:

I can read!

Note to Parents:

Sight words are a group of words that account for approximately 50% of all reading text. Understanding and recognizing these words by sight will allow beginner readers to focus on learning the remaining words in the text phonetically. Automatic recognition of these sight words leads to the mastery of reading.

One of the most common list of sight words is the Dolch Sight Word list first published in 1936. It is comprised of 220 service words and 95 common nouns. The list is divided into 5 parts : pre-primer, primer, first, second, and third.

This workbook focuses on the 52 words in the Dolch primer list. Repetition and memorization of these sight words is paramount to early reading skills. This workbook provides fun activities that will have a young reader saying, tracing, and writing each word. Also included is a section that provide flash cards that can be completed, cut out, and then laminated.

Encourage your child to take their time. This is meant to be a fun learning experience, so take breaks if needed. Follow their lead and use encouragement to create a life long learner!

Happy Learning!
Renee

Directions:

In each section focus on learning the handwriting strokes for both uppercase and lowercase letters. Learn to trace both. Trace with your finger first, then move on to tracing with a pencil or crayon. Practice pages are provided for both uppercase letters and lowercase letters.

Encourage your child to take their time. This is meant to be a fun learning experience, so take breaks if needed. Follow their lead and use encouragement to create a life long learner!

Sight Words
Pre-Primer

all	four	out	this
am	get	please	too
are	good	pretty	under
at	have	ran	want
ate	he	ride	was
be	into	saw	well
black	like	say	went
brown	must	she	what
but	new	so	white
came	no	soon	who
did	now	that	will
do	on	there	with
eat	our	they	yes

Learning Through Fun Activities

<u>Directions:</u>

Each page is filled with fun activities. These activities include coloring the sight word, saying the sight word, and writing the sight word. Other activities encourage learning through repetitions.

Track the process. After each page have the early learner color the designated sight word reward!

I can read!

Track the learning. After each page color your reward.

Track the learning. After each page color your reward.

must
new
no
now
on
our
out
please
pretty
ran
ride
saw
say
she
so
soon
that
there
they
this

Track the learning. After each page color your reward.

Sight Words

Say the word out loud.

Color It!

Trace the word.

Write the word.

Find the word in the sentence and circle it . Trace the word.

All of us went to the store.

I see all of the picture.

Write the missing word.

___ the cats meow for food.

I see ___ the girls.

Sight Words

Trace the word.

am

Write the word.

Find the word in the sentence and circle it . Trace the word.

I am at home.

Am I going to see you?

Write the missing word.

I __ hungry.

__ I ahead of you?

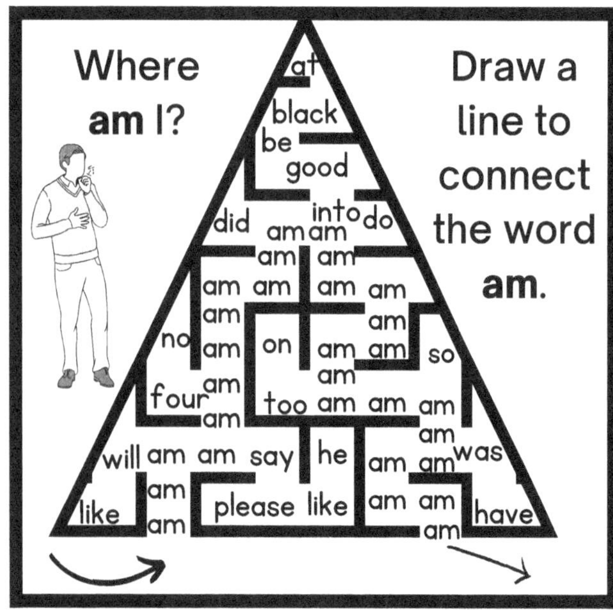

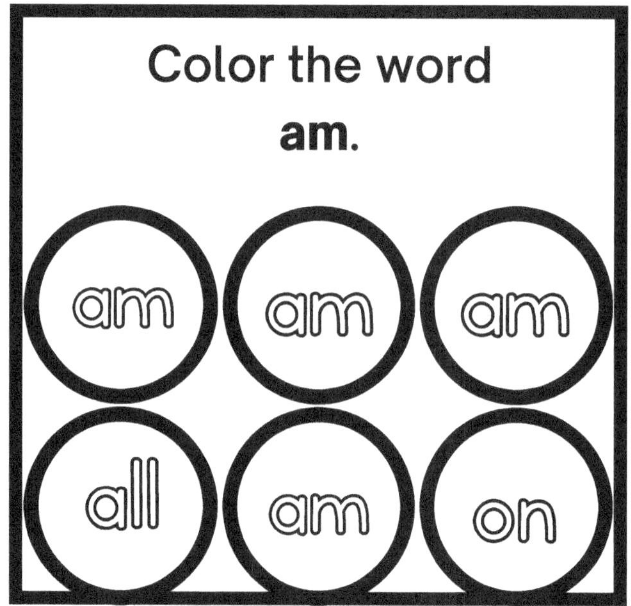

all

Trace the sight word:

all all all all all

Write the sight word:

am

Trace the sight word:

am am am am am

Write the sight word:

Sight Words

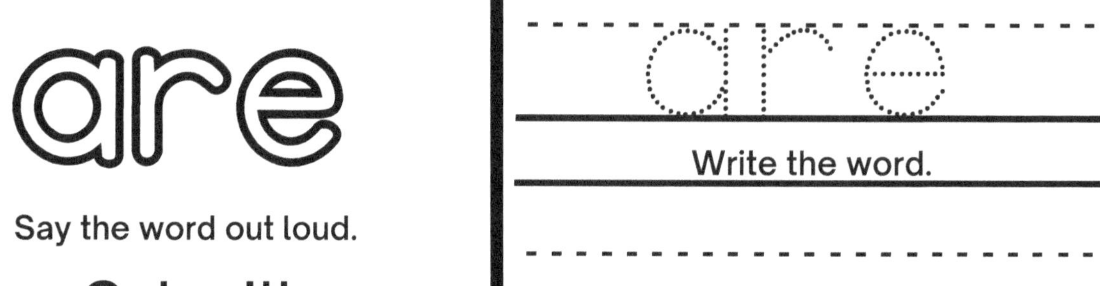

are

Say the word out loud.

Color It!

Write the word.

Find the word in the sentence and circle it . Trace the word.

We are going home.

The dogs are running fast.

Write the missing word.

The birds ___ singing. .

What ___ you doing?

Sight Words

Trace the word.

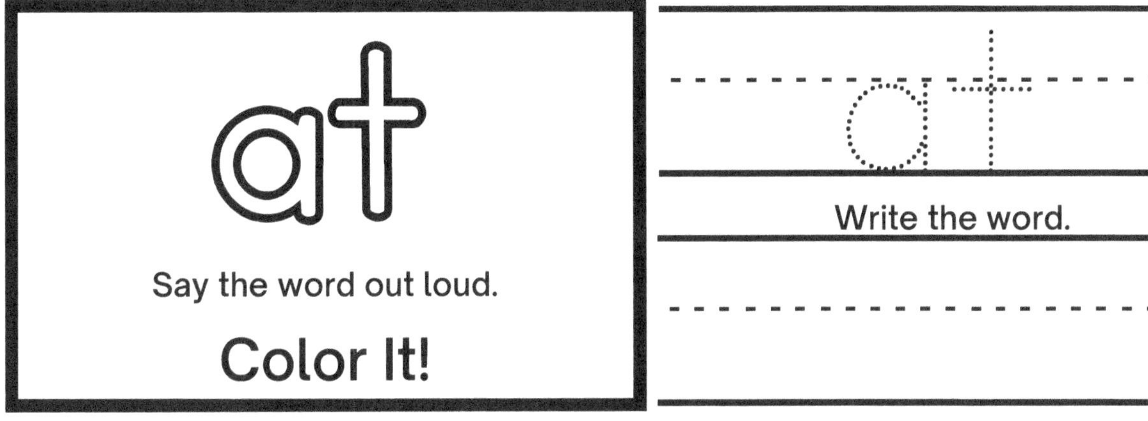

Write the word.

Find the word in the sentence and circle it . Trace the word.

The plane is at the airport.

My dad is at the store.

Write the missing word.

Look __ the mirror.

The cat is __ the vet's office.

Trace the sight word:

are are are are

Write the sight word:

at

Trace the sight word:

at at at at at

Write the sight word:

Sight Words

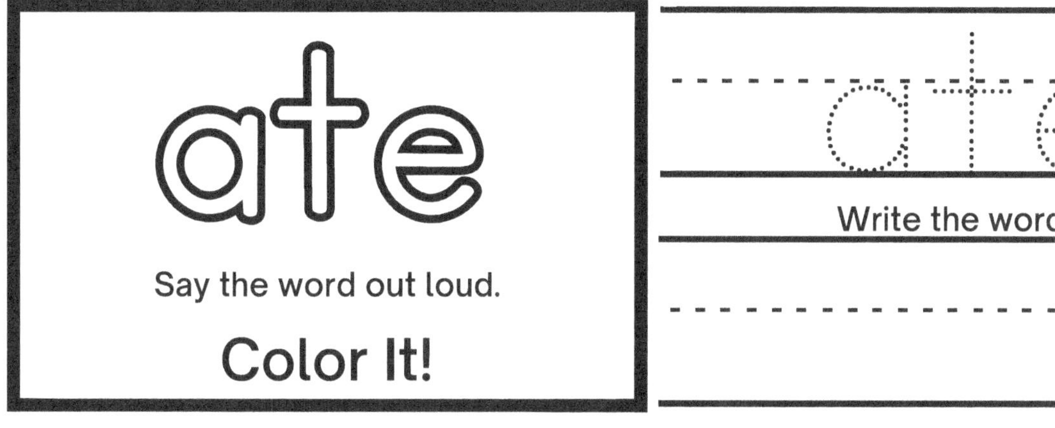

Find the word in the sentence and circle it . Trace the word.

I ate lunch with Nana.
I ate an apple.

Write the missing word.

The class ___ lunch together.
The dog ___ my sandwich.

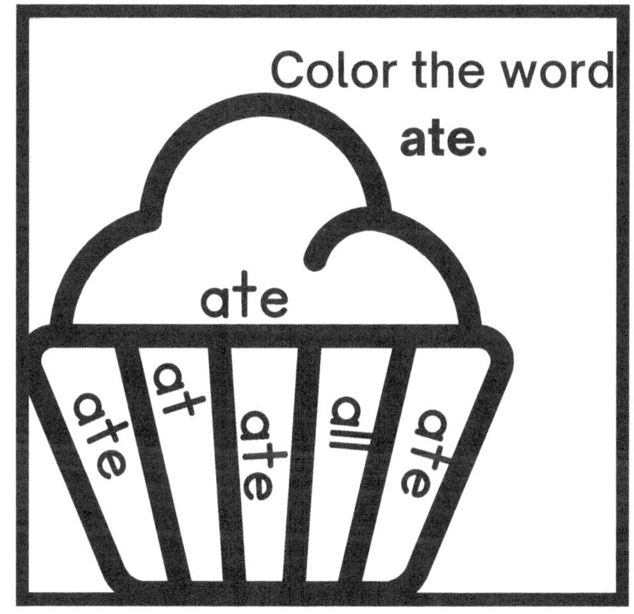

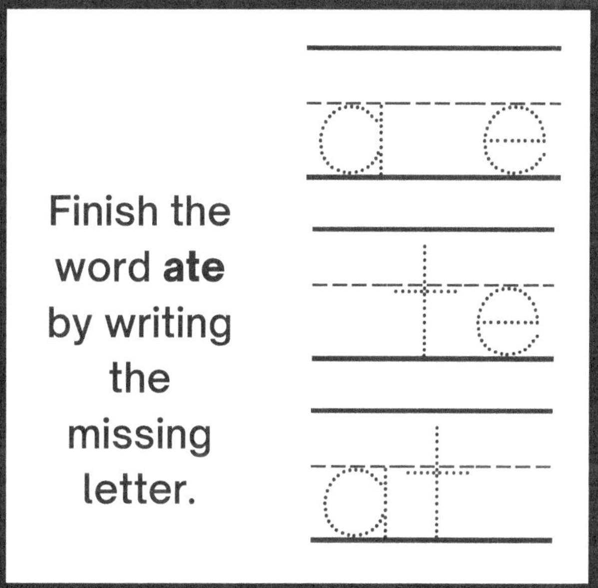

Finish the word **ate** by writing the missing letter.

Sight Words

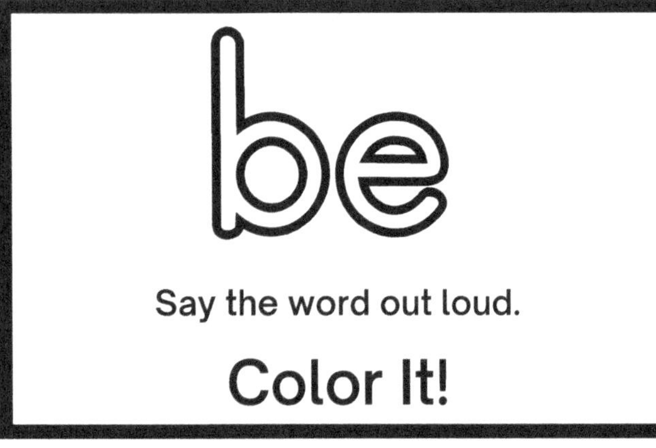

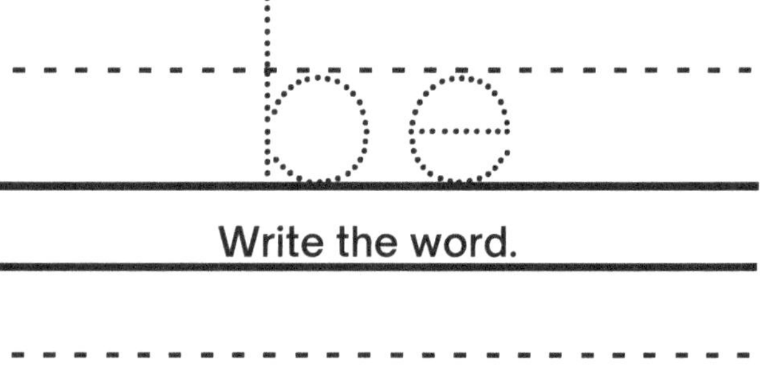

Find the word in the sentence and circle it . Trace the word.

I will be home later.

Birds can be loud.

Write the missing word.

We have to __ at school later.

When will you __ here?

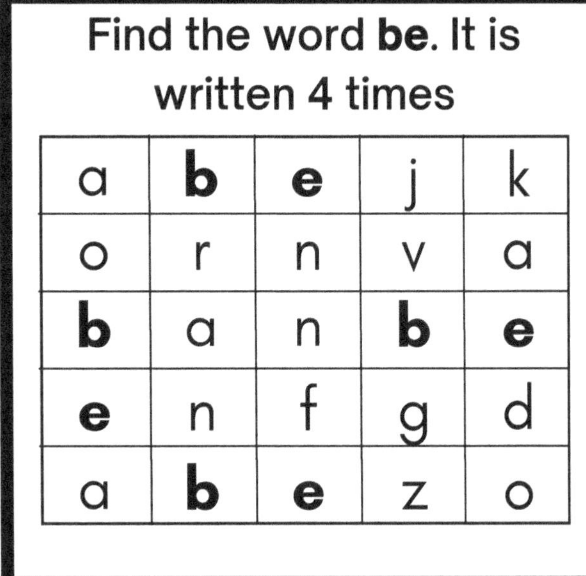

a	**b**	**e**	j	k
o	r	n	v	a
b	a	n	**b**	**e**
e	n	f	g	d
a	**b**	**e**	z	o

ate

Trace the sight word:

ate ate ate

Write the sight word:

be

Trace the sight word:

be be be be

Write the sight word:

Sight Words

black

Say the word out loud.

Color It!

Trace the word.

black

Write the word.

Find the word in the sentence and circle it . Trace the word.

Zebras are black and white.

The newspaper's ink is black.

Write the missing word.

They have _____ hair.
Write in _____ ink.

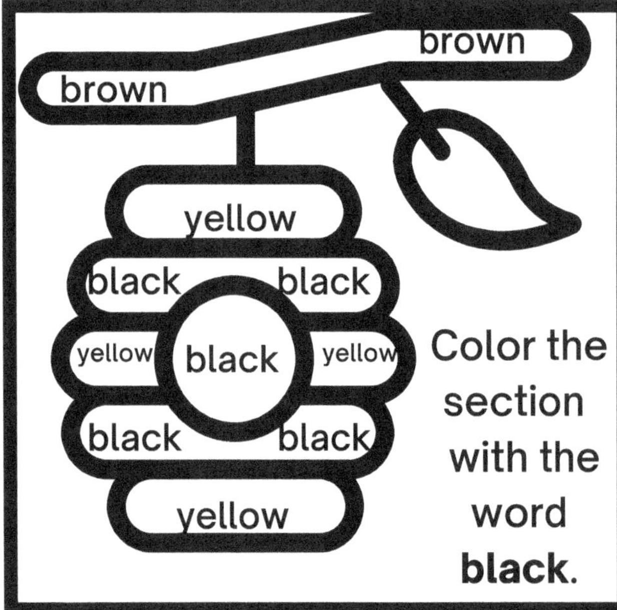

Color the section with the word **black**.

Sight Words

Say the word out loud.

Color It!

Write the word.

Find the word in the sentence and circle it . Trace the word.

The box is brown .
The girl has brown eyes.

Write the missing word.

The puppy has _____ fur.
My shoes are _____ .

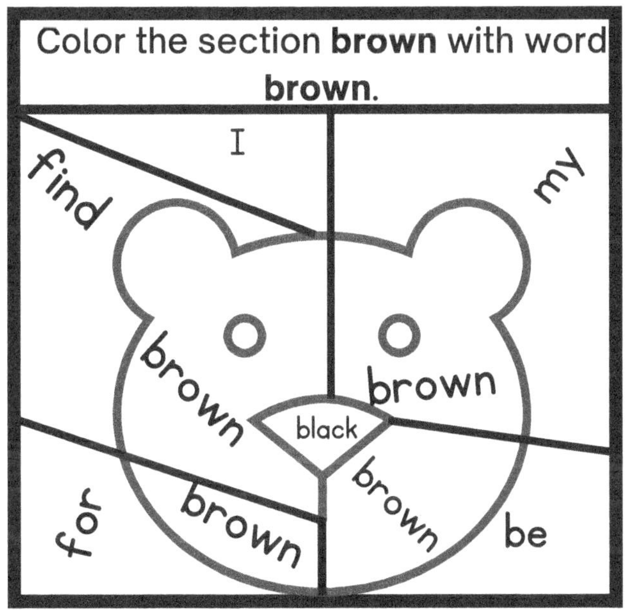

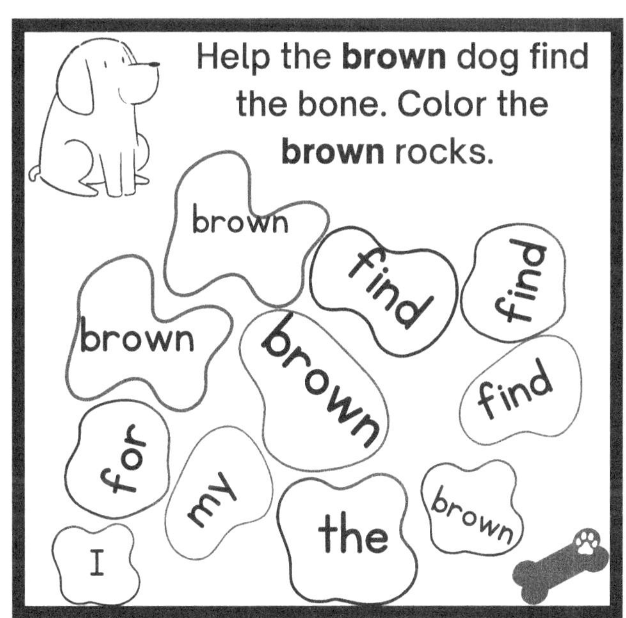

black

Trace the sight word:

black black

Write the sight word:

brown

Trace the sight word:

brown brown

Write the sight word:

Sight Words

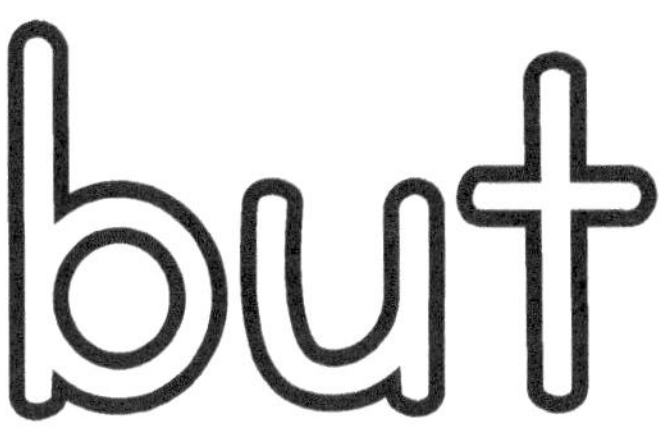

Say the word out loud.

Color It!

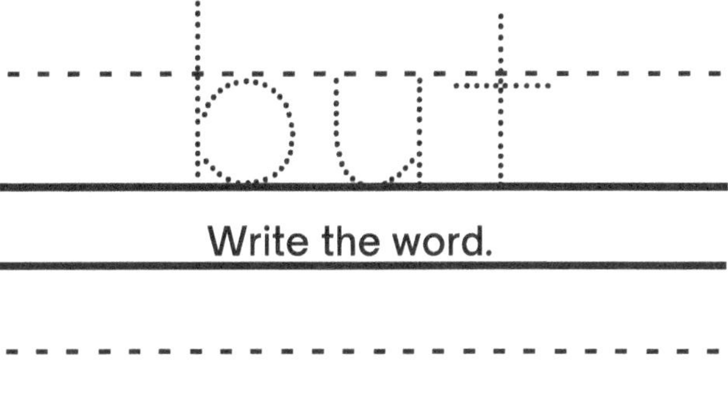

Write the word.

Find the word in the sentence and circle it . Trace the word.

I tried to stop but could not.
The day is beautiful but cold.

Write the missing word.

I can't, ___ Tom can go.
I have the lock ___ not the key.

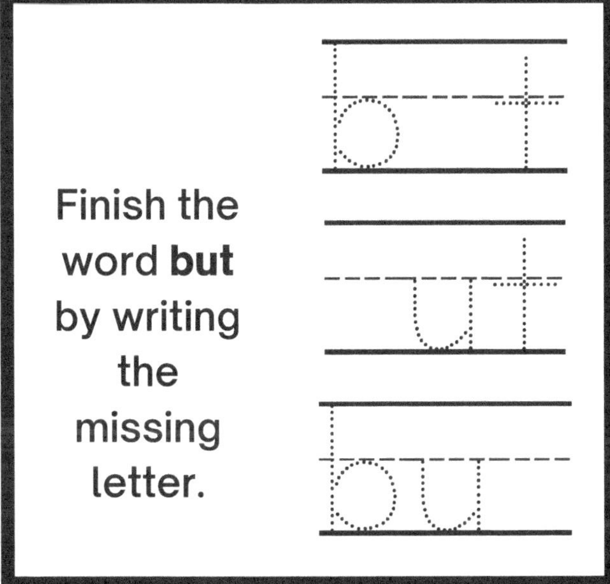

Finish the word **but** by writing the missing letter.

Draw a line to the matching **but**.

but
but
but

but

BUT

BUT
but

but
but

but

Sight Words

Find the word in the sentence and
circle it . Trace the word.

He came with me to the store .

The bus came to pick us up.

Write the missing word.

The box ____ in the mail .

She ____ to eat with us.

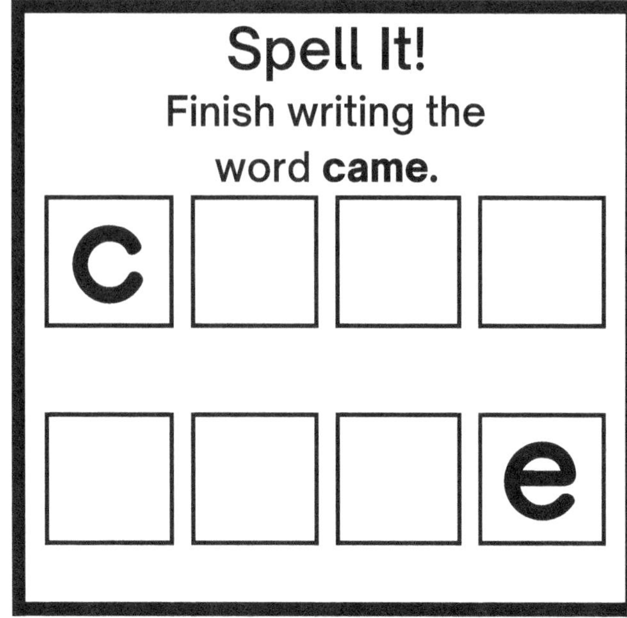

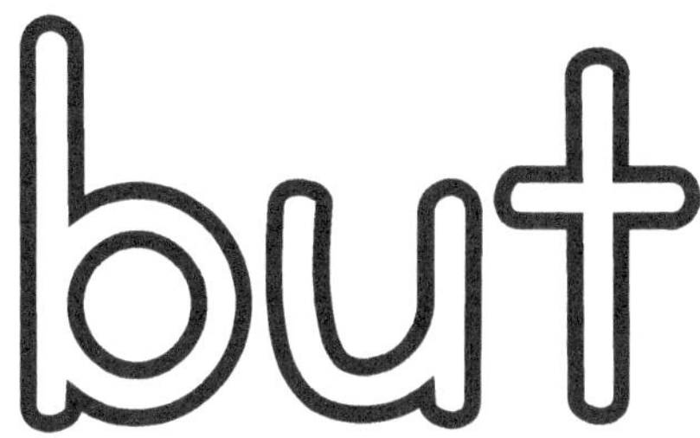

but

Trace the sight word:

but but but

Write the sight word:

came

Trace the sight word:

came came

Write the sight word:

Sight Words

Find the word in the sentence and
circle it . Trace the word.

Did you know the answer?

He did his homework.

Write the missing word.

That is what he ___ .

What ___ she say?

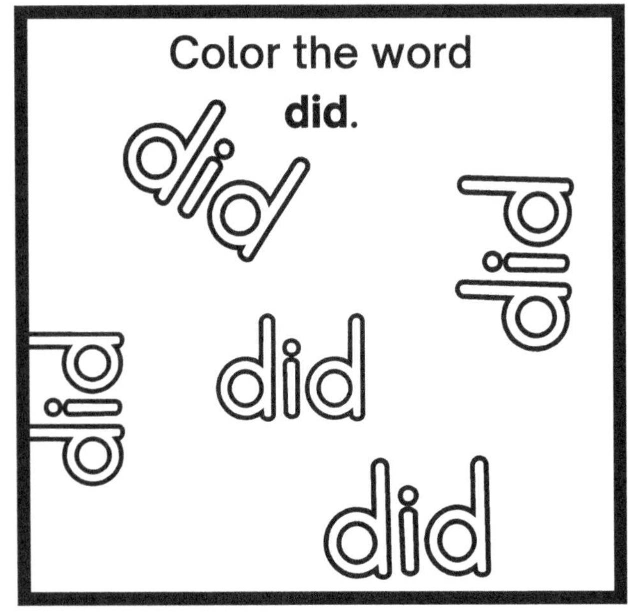

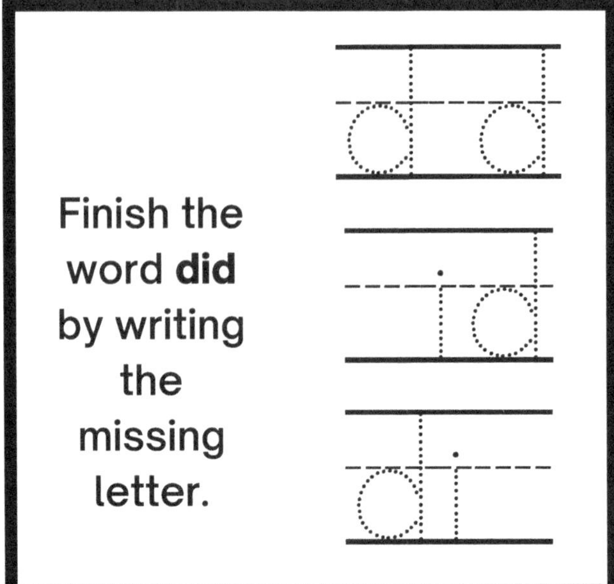

Sight Words

Find the word in the sentence and circle it . Trace the word.

We should do that again.
Do not let him out.

Write the missing word.

I have to __ my homework.
Where __ they live?

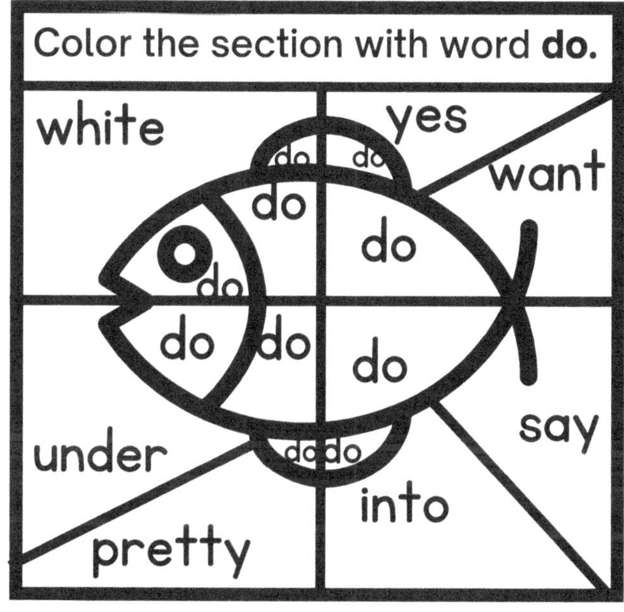

Trace the sight word:

Write the sight word:

do

Trace the sight word:

Write the sight word:

Sight Words

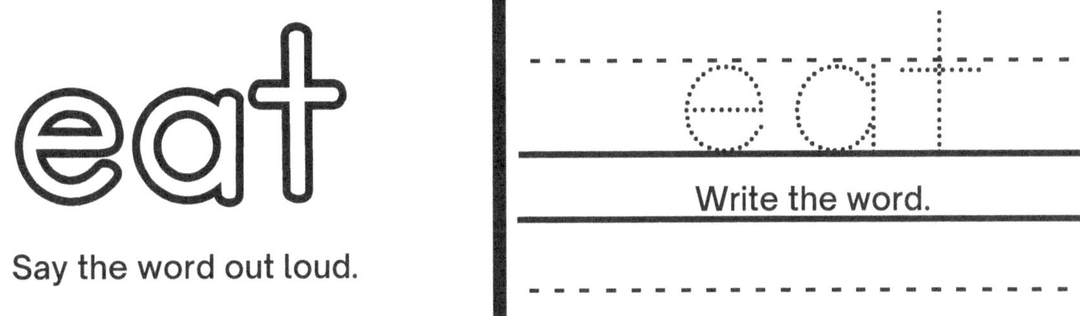

Say the word out loud.

Color It!

Trace the word.

Write the word.

Find the word in the sentence and circle it . Trace the word.

We should eat now.
Let her eat her food.

Write the missing word.

I have to ___ lunch still.
Where did you ___ lunch?

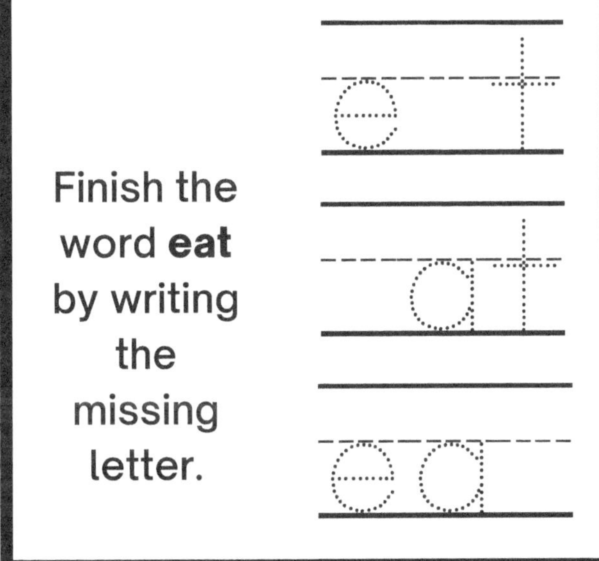

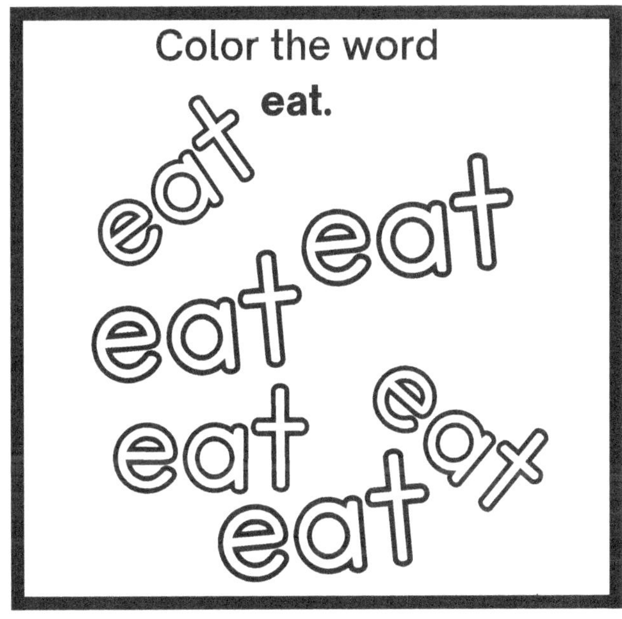

Sight Words

four

Say the word out loud.

Color It!

Trace the word.

four

Write the word.

Find the word in the sentence and circle it . Trace the word.

Maddie is four years old.
She got four boxes in the mail.

Write the missing word.

There are ____ cakes.

Why do you need ____ balls?

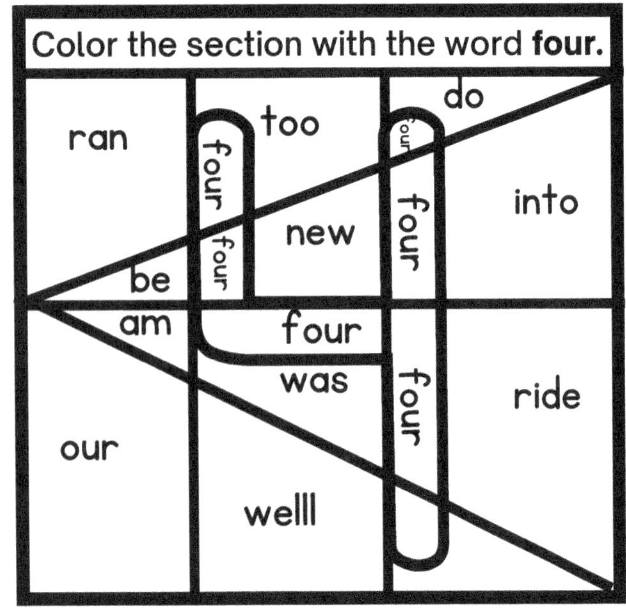

Trace the sight word:

eat eat eat

Write the sight word:

four

Trace the sight word:

four four

Write the sight word:

Sight Words

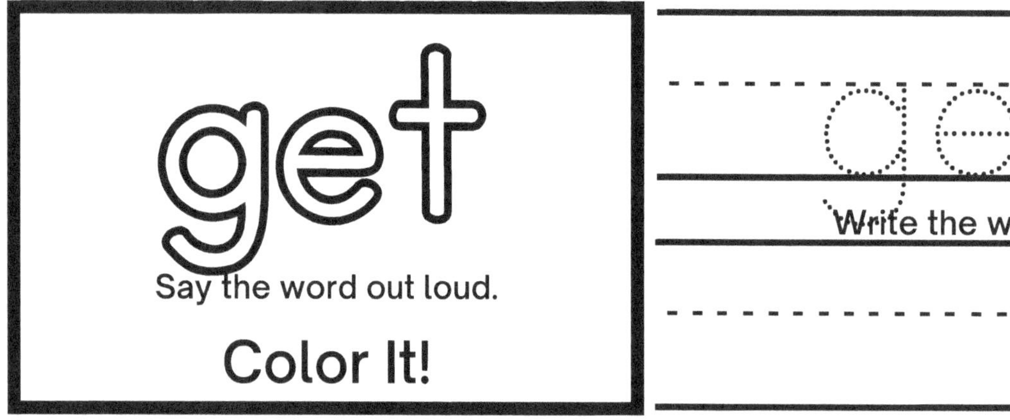

Find the word in the sentence and circle it . Trace the word.

I am here to get the pie.
How do I get there?

Write the missing word.

___ help!
What do I ___ for you?

Sight Words

Say the word out loud.

Color It!

Trace the word.

Write the word.

Find the word in the sentence and circle it . Trace the word.

He did good on the test.
The food tasted good .

Write the missing word.

Kate was ____ at school.
Is the music ____ ?

Unscramble the word **good**. Write below.

Spell It!
Finish writing the word **good**.

g

d

get

Trace the sight word:

get get get

Write the sight word:

good

Trace the sight word:

good good

Write the sight word:

Sight Words

Say the word out loud.

Color It!

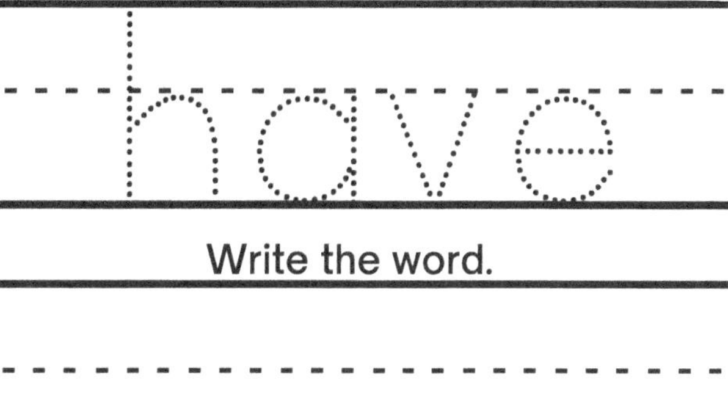

Write the word.

Find the word in the sentence and circle it . Trace the word.

I have the box.

What do you have ?

Write the missing word.

You ____ a dog

____ you tried the cake?

Find and circle the word **have**. It is written 4 times

h	a	v	e	k
a	r	h	v	h
v	a	a	d	a
e	n	v	g	v
a	h	e	z	e

Unscramble the word **have**. Write below.

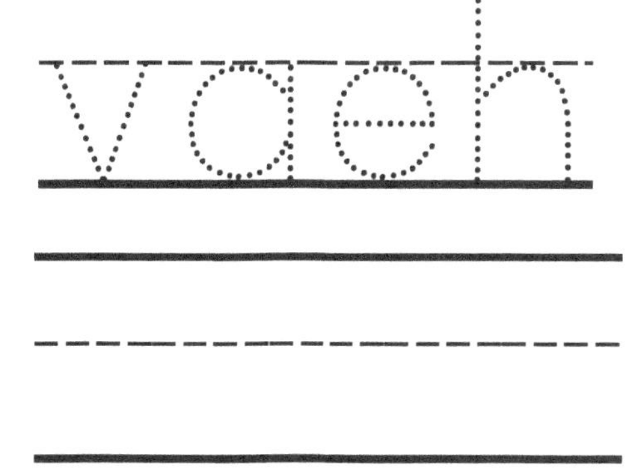

Sight Words

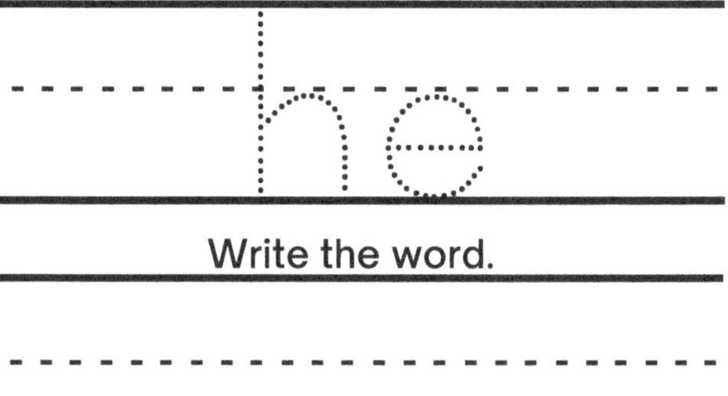

Find the word in the sentence and circle it . Trace the word.

He likes turtles.

What does he want?

Write the missing word.

__ has a dog.

Has __ tried the cake?

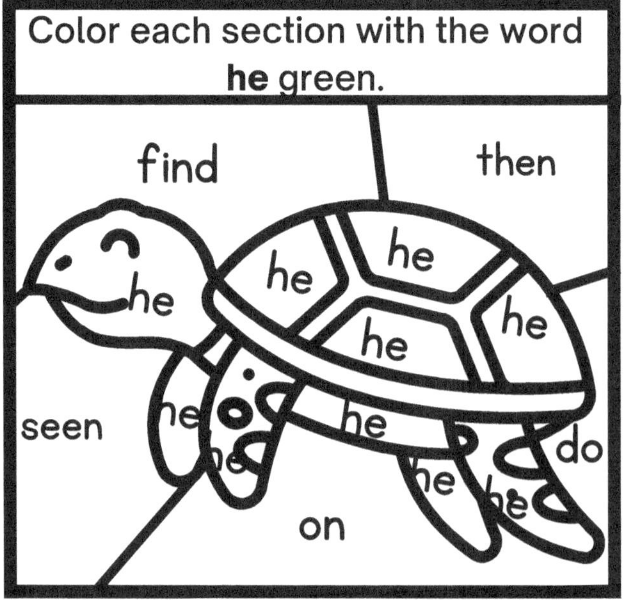

Trace the sight word:

have have

Write the sight word:

he

Trace the sight word:

he he he he

Write the sight word:

Sight Words

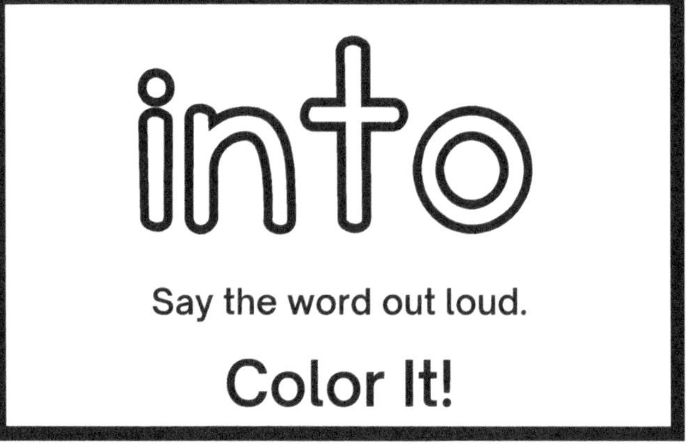

Say the word out loud.

Color It!

Trace the word.

Write the word.

Find the word in the sentence and circle it . Trace the word.

Frogs jumped into the pond.
The boy went into the house.

Write the missing word.

Jack lead them ____ the bus.
He wanted ____ the house?

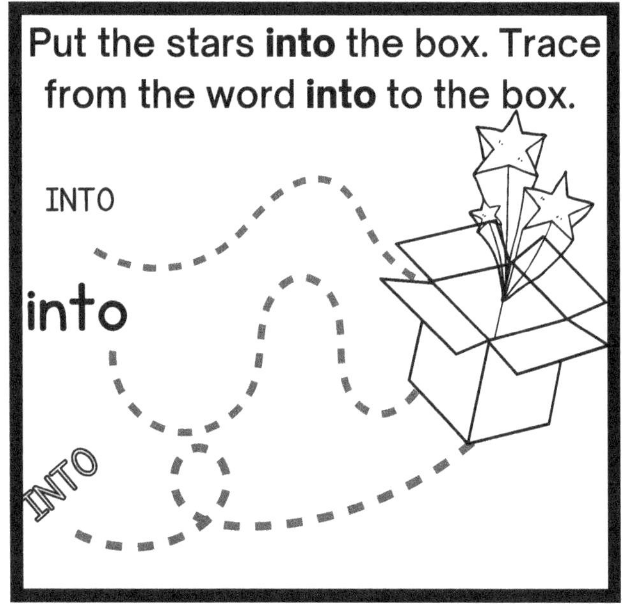

Sight Words

like

Say the word out loud.

Color It!

Write the word.

Find the word in the sentence and circle it . Trace the word.

Some bugs like to bite.

They like to talk.

Write the missing word.

Jane did not ____ the cake.

Do you ____ candy?

Spell It!
Finish writing the word **like.**

l			

			e

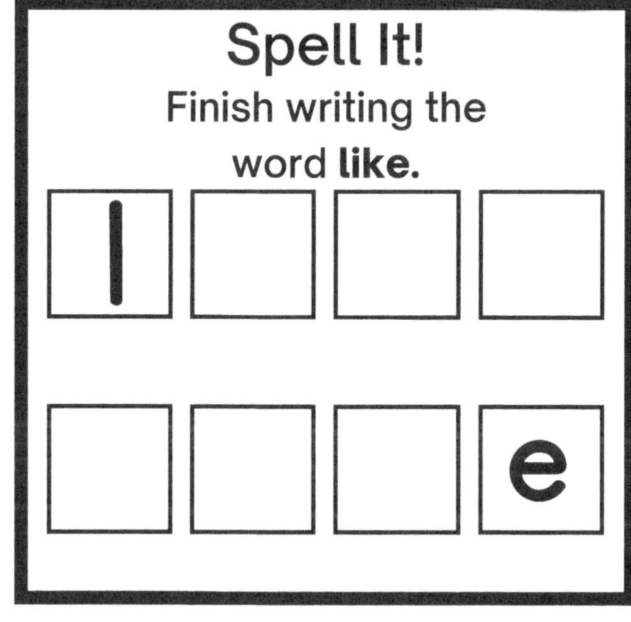

into

Trace the sight word:

into into into into

Write the sight word:

like

Trace the sight word:

like like like

Write the sight word:

Sight Words

must

Say the word out loud.

Color It!

Trace the word.

Write the word.

Find the word in the sentence and circle it . Trace the word.

Sarah must wear a hat.

Must we read the book?

Write the missing word.

You ____ read the book.

We ____ not be late.

Spell It!

Finish writing the word **must**.

m			
			t

Unscramble the word **must**. Write below.

tums

Sight Words

Say the word out loud.

Color It!

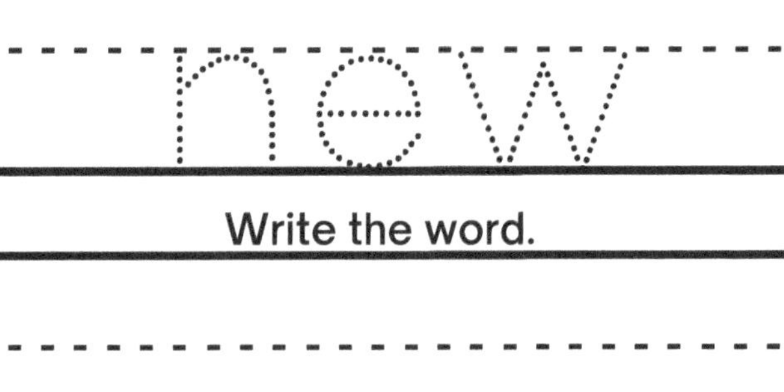

Write the word.

Find the word in the sentence and circle it . Trace the word.

I am new here.

I have a new boy in my class.

Write the missing word.

You can buy a ___ car.

Do you have a ___ cat?

Draw a line to the matching **new.**

new   NEW
new   new
new   new
new   new
NEW   new

Trace the word

new.

Trace the sight word:

must must

Write the sight word:

new

Trace the sight word:

new new new

Write the sight word:

Sight Words

Say the word out loud.

Color It!

Trace the word.

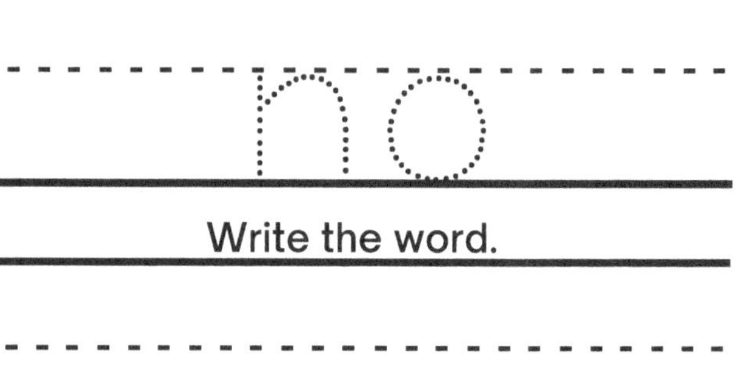

Write the word.

Find the word in the sentence and circle it . Trace the word.

There are  no stairs.

David said no .

Write the missing word.

There is __ candy left.

Did she say __ ?

Complete the word **no** by tracing the letters.

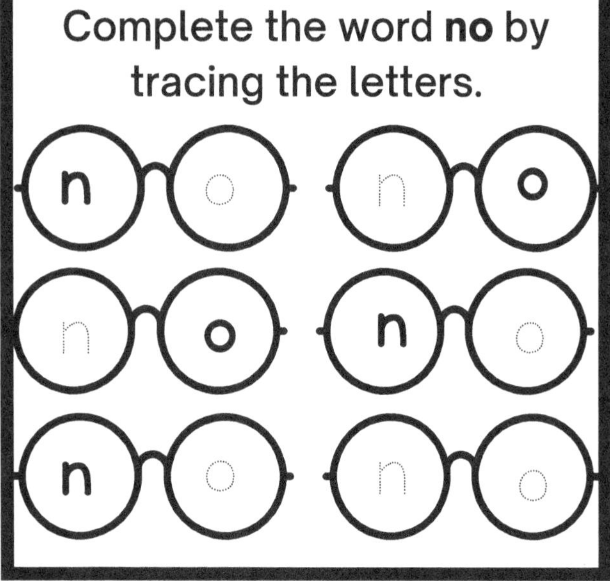

Find the word **no** It is written 4 times

a	**n**	**o**	j	k
o	r	n	v	a
n	a	n	**n**	**o**
n	n	f	g	d
a	**n**	**o**	**n**	**o**

Sight Words

Trace the word.

now

Write the word.

Find the word in the sentence and circle it . Trace the word.

You are now home.

Give me the ball now .

Write the missing word.

I feel better ___ .

___ I can say I am finished?

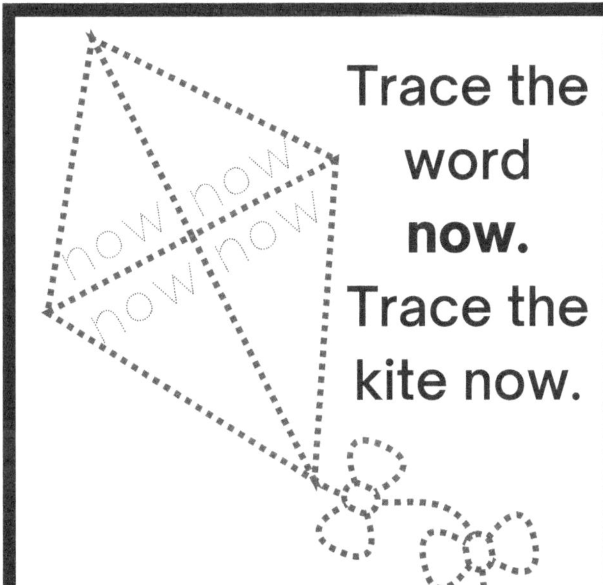

Trace the word **now.** Trace the kite now.

Unscramble the word **now.** Write below.

wno

no

Trace the sight word:

no no no no

Write the sight word:

now

Trace the sight word:

now now now

Write the sight word:

Sight Words

Trace the word.

Write the word.

Find the word in the sentence and circle it . Trace the word.

He is on the swing.

I left my book on the bus.

Write the missing word.

Tillie went __ an airplane.

What is going __ ?

Sight Words

Say the word out loud.

Color It!

Write the word.

Find the word in the sentence and circle it . Trace the word.

We gave our toys away.
This is our ball.

Write the missing word.

You can give ___ cake away.
Do you want ___ help?

Draw a line to the matching **our.**

our
our
our
our
OUR

OUR
our
our
our
our

Finish the word **our** by writing the missing letter.

on

Trace the sight word:

on on on on on

Write the sight word:

our

Trace the sight word:

our our our

Write the sight word:

Sight Words

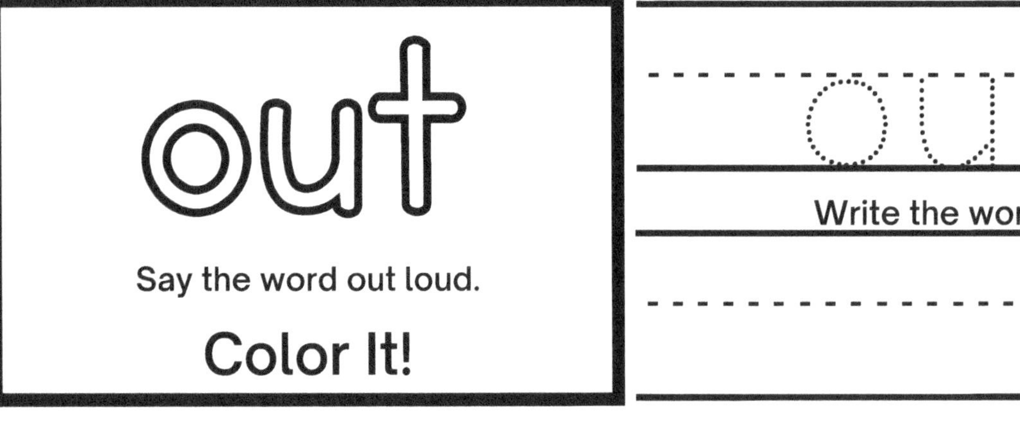

Say the word out loud.

Color It!

Trace the word.

Write the word.

Find the word in the sentence and circle it . Trace the word.

They store was out of milk.

Maddie held out her hand.

Write the missing word.

You can go __ the door.

Do you want to ___ to play?

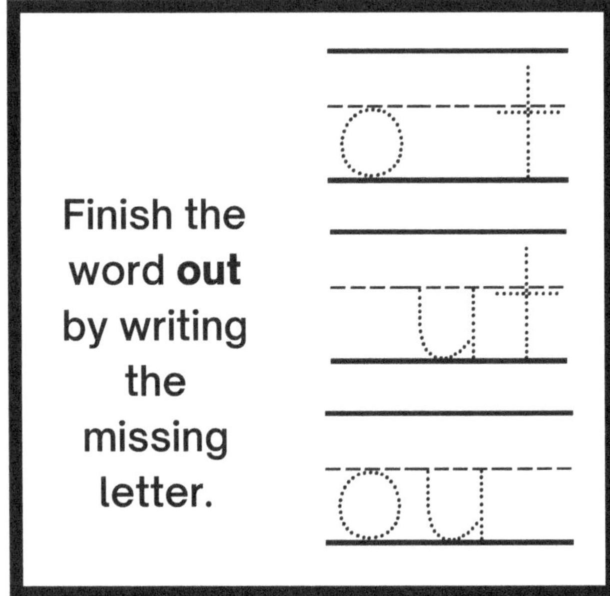

Finish the word **out** by writing the missing letter.

Draw a line to the matching **out**.

out   OUT

out   out

out   out

out   out

OUT   out

Sight Words

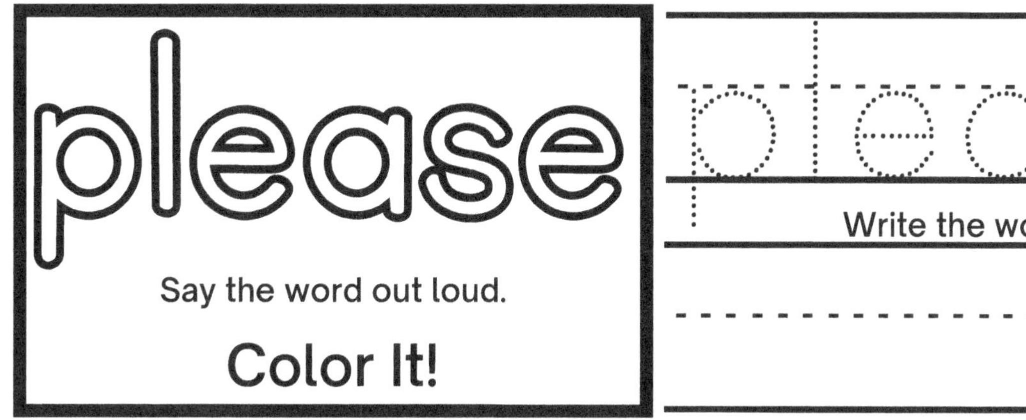

please

Say the word out loud.

Color It!

Trace the word.

please

Write the word.

Find the word in the sentence and circle it . Trace the word.

Please help clean up.

Follow me please.

Write the missing word.

You can do as you _______ .

_______ give this to your dad?

Please help. Color the circles with the letters in the word **please.**

P	L	R	Y
B	E	A	Z
U	C	S	O
D	T	E	K

Trace the sight word:

out out out

Write the sight word:

please

Trace the sight word:

please please

Write the sight word:

Sight Words

pretty

Say the word out loud.

Color It!

Write the word.

Find the word in the sentence and circle it . Trace the word.

The flower is pretty.

Jane drew a pretty picture.

Write the missing word.

The bird had ______ features.

How ______ was the picture?

Color the section of the picture with the word **pretty**.

Sight Words

Trace the word.

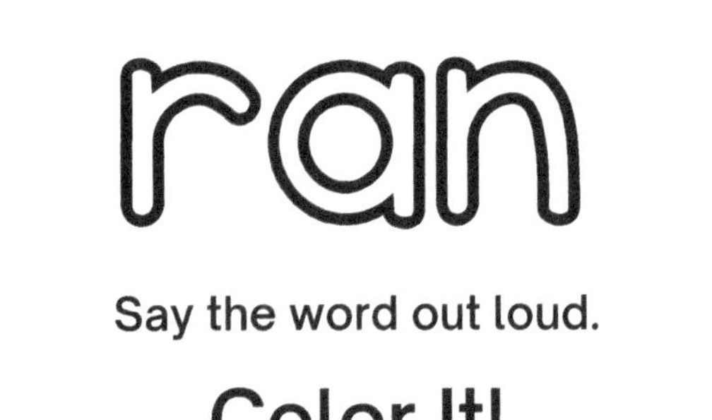

Say the word out loud.

Color It!

Write the word.

Find the word in the sentence and circle it . Trace the word.

I ran **fast.**

The fox ran **away.**

Write the missing word.

You ___ fast .

The boy ___ up the stairs.

Draw a line to the matching **ran.**

ran

ran

ran

ran

RAN

RAN

ran

ran

ran

ran

Finish the word **ran** by writing the missing letter.

pretty

Trace the sight word:

pretty pretty pretty

Write the sight word:

ran

Trace the sight word:

ran ran ran

Write the sight word:

Sight Words

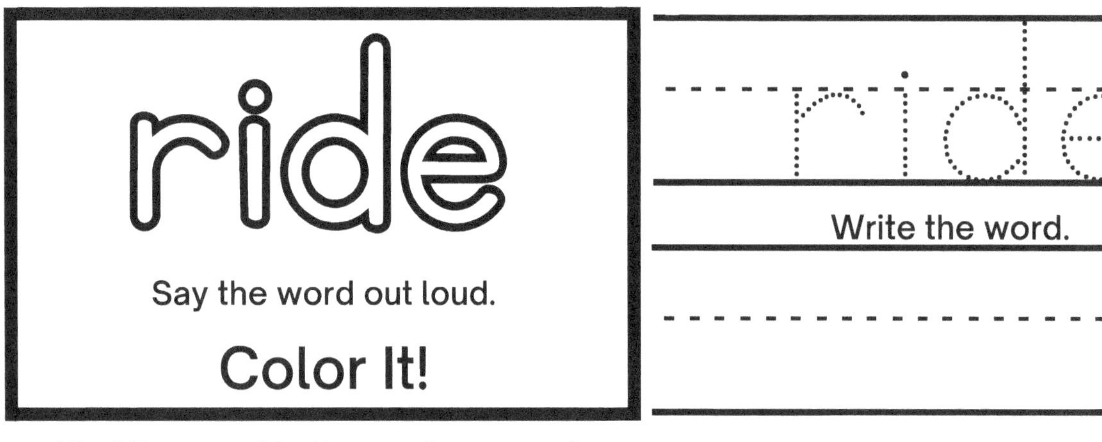

Find the word in the sentence and circle it . Trace the word.

I ride the bus to school.

Allyson could ride the bike.

Write the missing word.

She can ____ the elephant.

Can you ____ the horse?

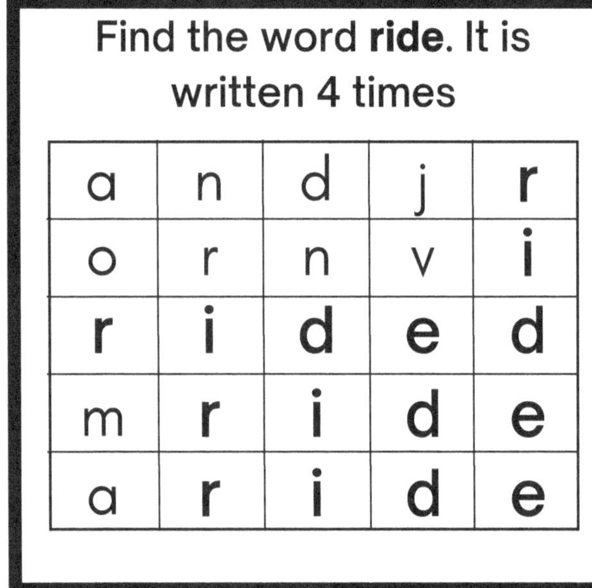

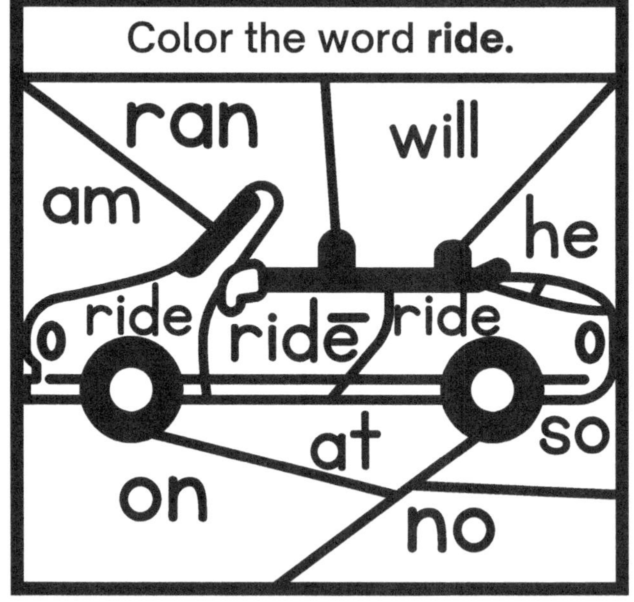

Sight Words

Trace the word.

saw

Say the word out loud.

Color It!

Trace the word.

Write the word.

Find the word in the sentence and
circle it . Trace the word.

We saw the lion at the zoo.

Jason saw a movie.

Write the missing word.

She ___ him cross the finish line.

Who ___ the movie with Jason?

Trace the
word **saw**.

Unscramble the word **saw**.
Write below.

swa

ride

Trace the sight word:

see see see

Write the sight word:

saw

Trace the sight word:

the the the

Write the sight word:

Sight Words

Say the word out loud.

Color It!

Trace the word.

Write the word.

Find the word in the sentence and circle it . Trace the word.

Say that again please.

I won't say anything else.

Write the missing word.

He had to ___ goodbye.

What did she ___ ?

Sight Words

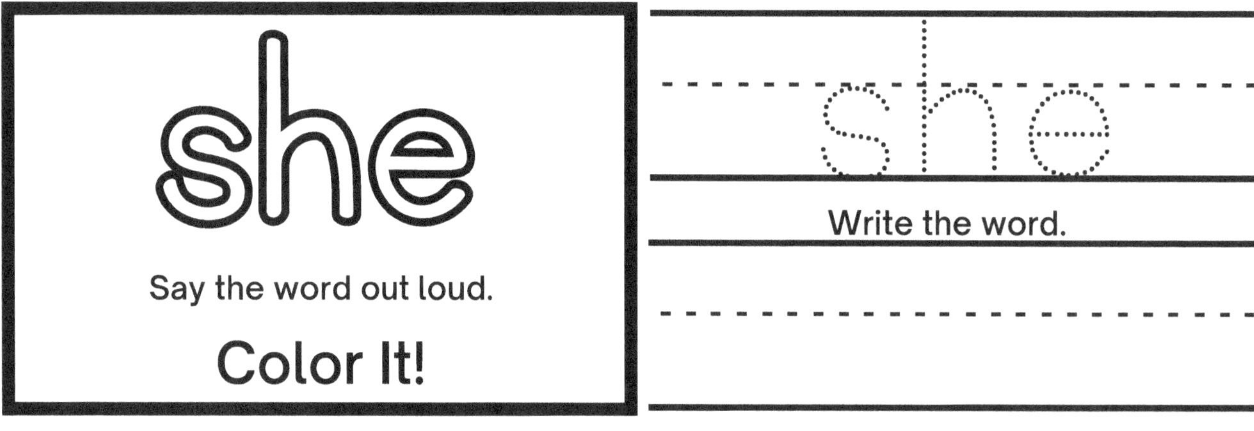

Find the word in the sentence and
circle it . Trace the word.

She is going to school.
What did she bake?

Write the missing word.

___ went for a ride.
Did ___ want to go fishing?

Finish the
word she
by writing
the
missing
letter.

say

Trace the sight word:

say say say

Write the sight word:

she

Trace the sight word:

she she she

Write the sight word:

Sight Words

Say the word out loud.

Color It!

Trace the word.

SO

Write the word.

Find the word in the sentence and circle it . Trace the word.

I love you so much.

Roger won so many prizes.

Write the missing word.

It wasn't __ bad.

Let's finish __ we can go.

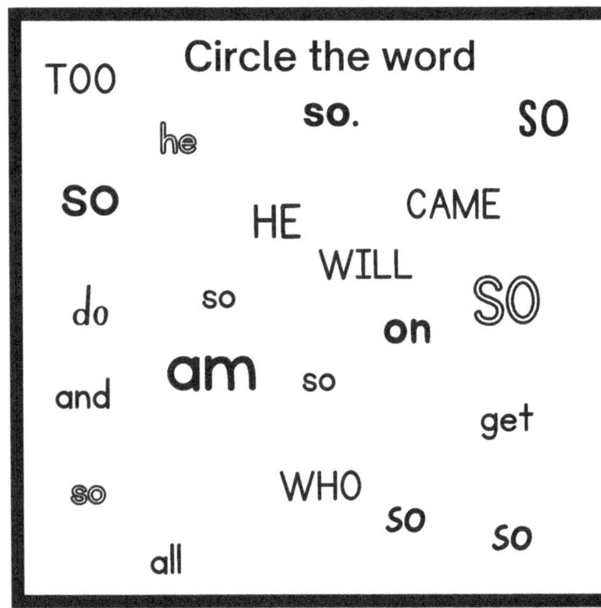

Sight Words

Say the word out loud.

Color It!

Trace the word.

Write the word.

Find the word in the sentence and circle it . Trace the word.

Soon **we can eat lunch.**

David will be home soon .

Write the missing word.

I have to go ____ .

Do you need to go ____ ?

Find the word soon. It is written 4 times

a	n	d	j	s
o	r	n	v	o
s	o	o	n	o
m	s	o	o	n
a	s	o	o	n

Draw a line to the matching **soon.**

Soon

soon

soon

soon

SOON

SOON

soon

Soon

soon

soon

 SO

Trace the sight word:

SO SO SO SO

Write the sight word:

soon

Trace the sight word:

soon soon

Write the sight word:

Sight Words

Say the word out loud.

Color It!

Trace the word.

Write the word.

Find the word in the sentence and circle it . Trace the word.

That toy is mine.

I wish that I had more time.

Write the missing word.

Did you do ____ ?

____ was fun.

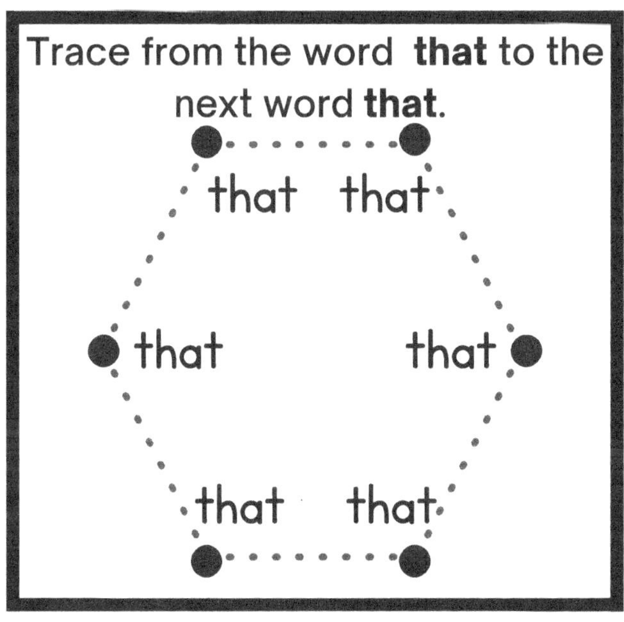

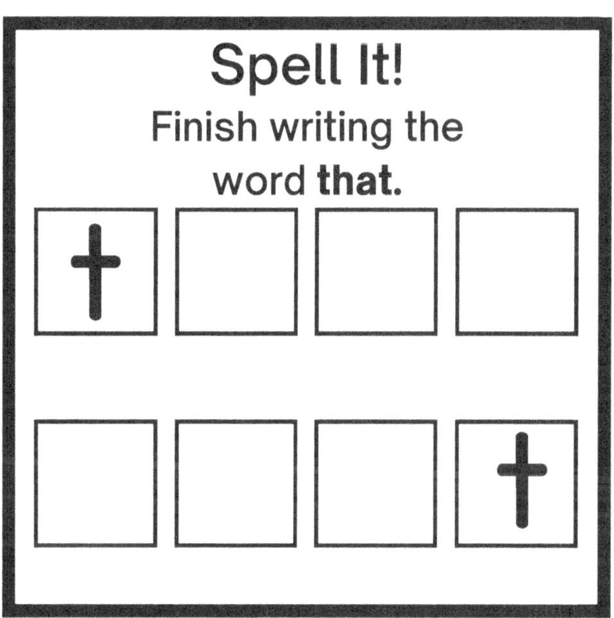

Sight Words

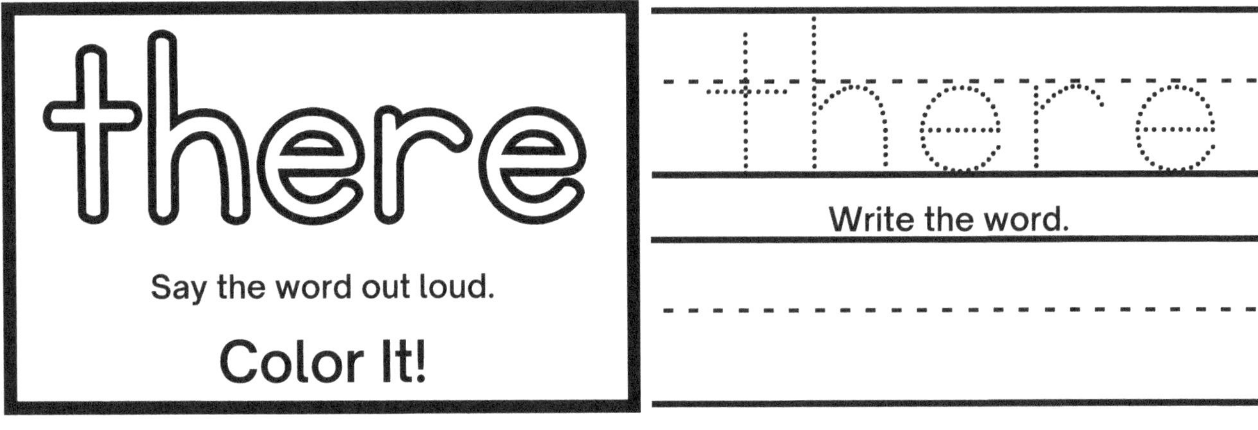

there

Say the word out loud.

Color It!

Write the word.

Find the word in the sentence and circle it . Trace the word.

Is there any candy left?

There is a dog in my chair.

Write the missing word.

I went _____ for a visit.

Did you know I live ______ ?

Write the word **there** on the candy.

Unscramble the word **there**. Write below.

tehre

that

Trace the sight word:

that that that

Write the sight word:

there

Trace the sight word

there there there

Write the sight word:

Sight Words

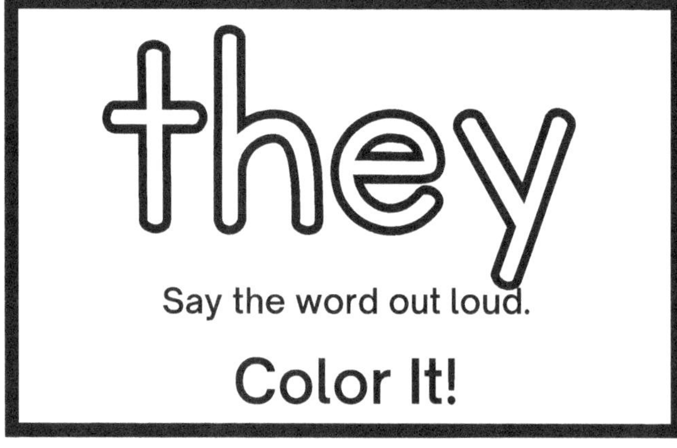

Write the word.

Find the word in the sentence and circle it . Trace the word.

I wish they had made a pie.

They are home.

Write the missing word.

This is the school bus ____ ride.

____ like bananas.

Circle the banana with the word **they**.

Circle the word **they**.

Sight Words

Say the word out loud.

Color It!

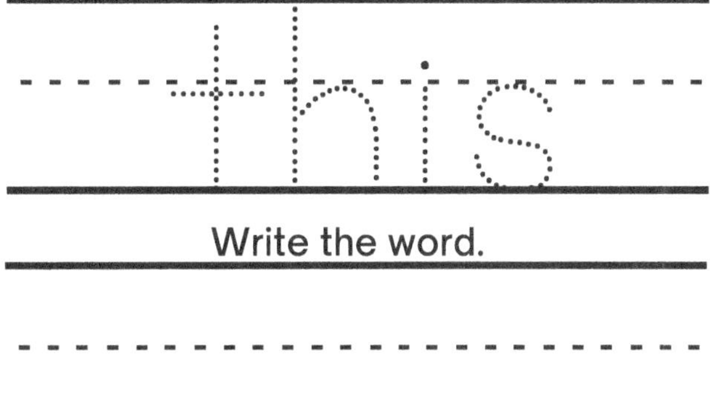

Write the word.

Find the word in the sentence and circle it . Trace the word.

This is my favorite food.

I can see this.

Write the missing word.

____ makes me smile.

Do you like ____ ?

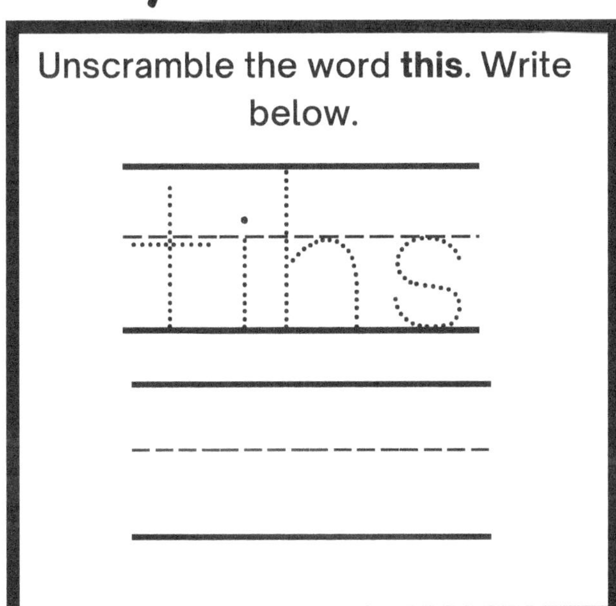

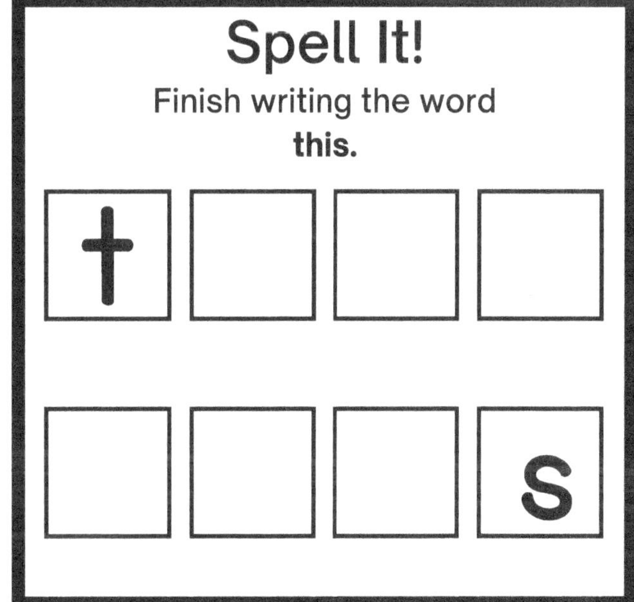

Trace the sight word:

they they they

Write the sight word:

this

Trace the sight word:

this this this

Write the sight word:

Sight Words

Say the word out loud.

Color It!

Trace the word.

too

Write the word.

Find the word in the sentence and
circle it . Trace the word.

Love you too.

It is too far to go.

Write the missing word.

It is never ___ late.

Do you want to go ___ ?

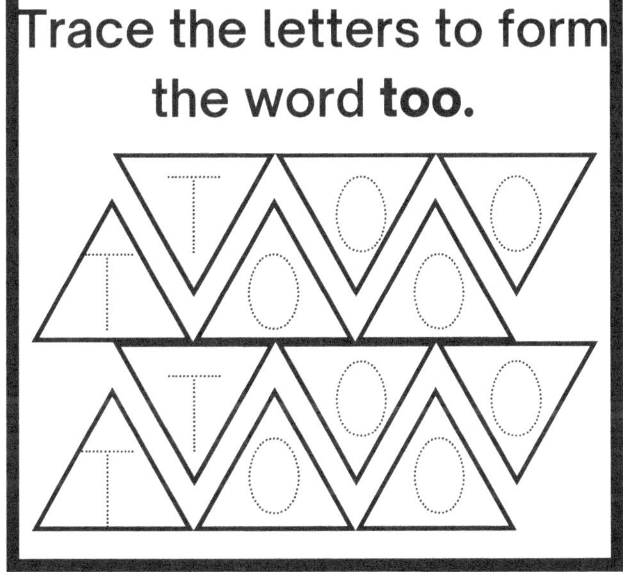

Trace the letters to form
the word **too.**

Find the word **too**. It is
written 4 times

w	x	t	h	t
t	o	o	v	o
t	k	o	m	o
o	z	b	d	h
o	p	h	c	e

Sight Words

Trace the word.

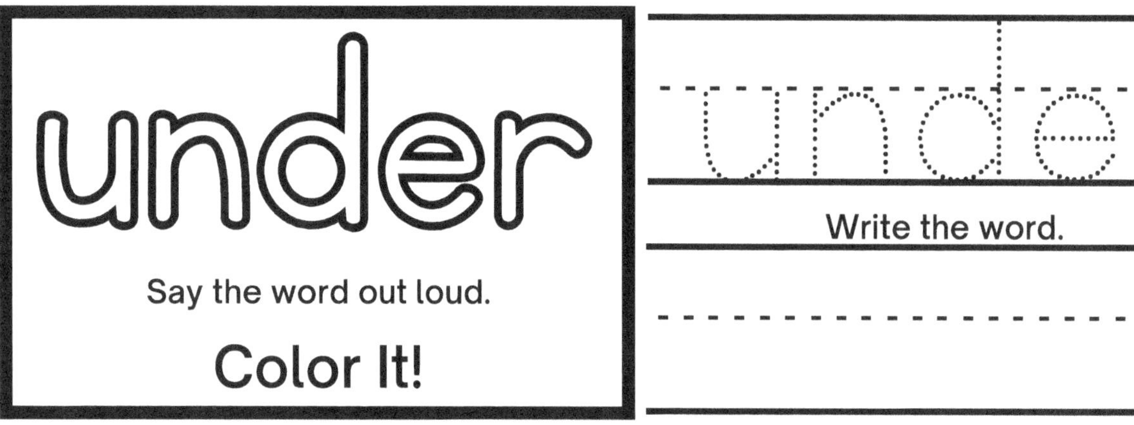

Say the word out loud.

Color It!

Write the word.

Find the word in the sentence and circle it . Trace the word.

We sat under the tree.

I can see under the water.

Write the missing word.

_____ the tree sat three boys.

Are you _____ the tree?

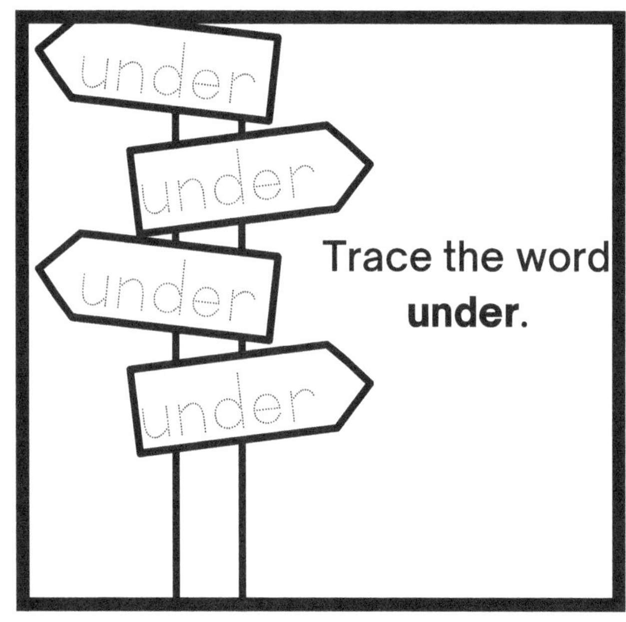

Trace the word **under**.

Color the word **under**.

too

Trace the sight word:

too   too   too

Write the sight word:

under

Trace the sight word:

under   under

Write the sight word:

Sight Words

Trace the word.

Write the word.

Find the word in the sentence and circle it . Trace the word.

We want to play outside.

I want go to the store.

Write the missing word.

I _____ him to be happy.

Do you _____ the toy?

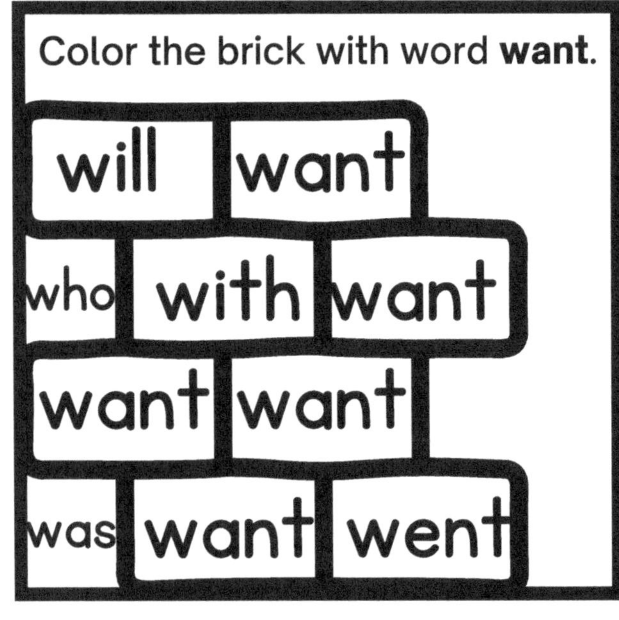

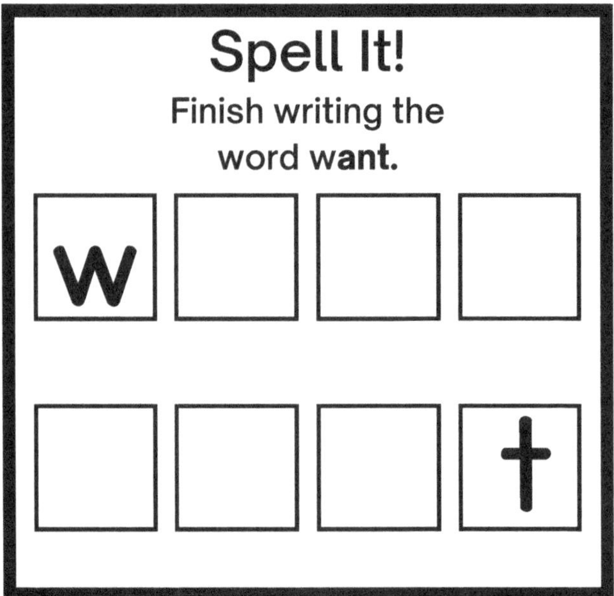

Sight Words

Say the word out loud.

Color It!

Trace the word.

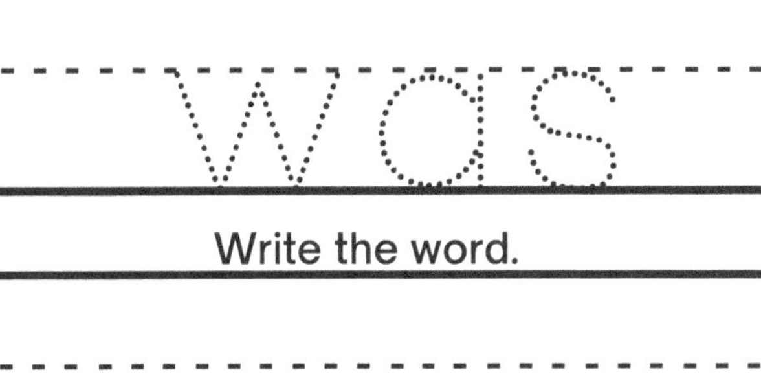

Write the word.

Find the word in the sentence and circle it . Trace the word.

She was looking out the window.

He was riding the bus home.

Write the missing word.

The book ___ good.

Where ___ the boy?

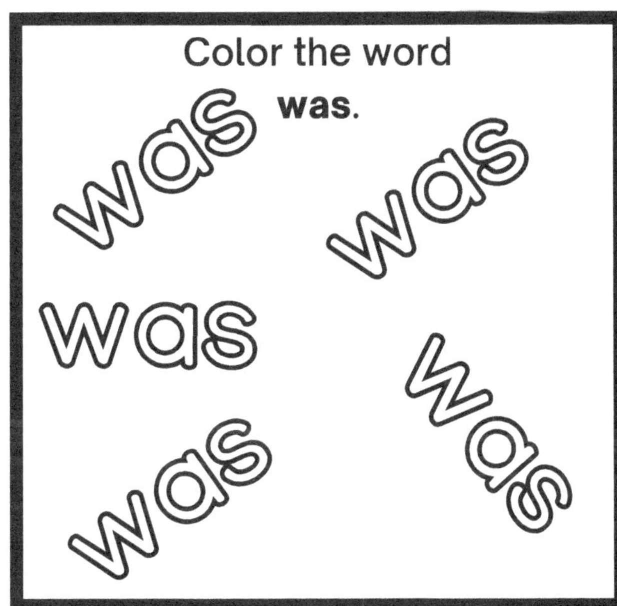

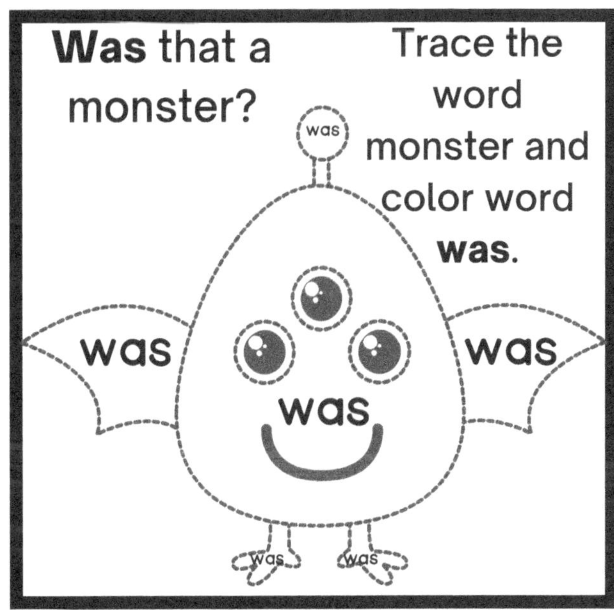

Trace the sight word:

Write the sight word:

was

Trace the sight word:

Write the sight word:

Sight Words

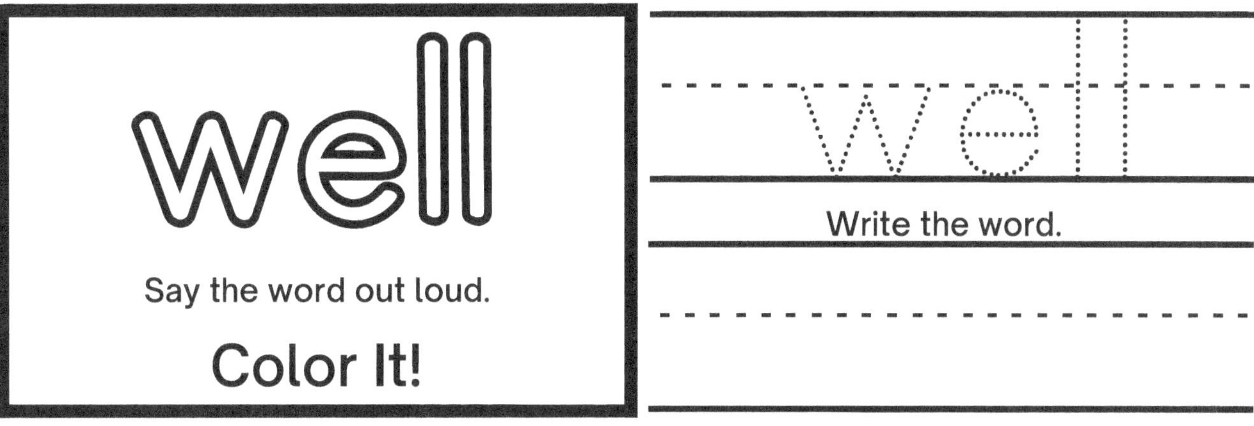

Find the word in the sentence and
circle it . Trace the word.

I hope the race went well.

He rides the bus home as well .

Write the missing word.

_____ , let us go now.

Is he going as _____ ?

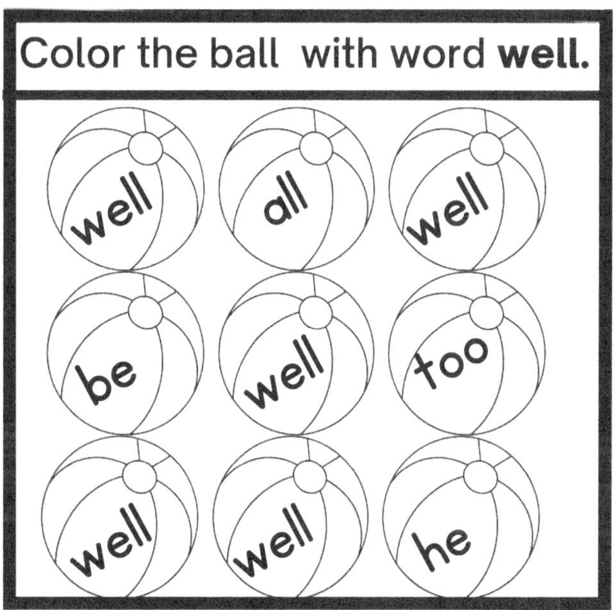

Sight Words

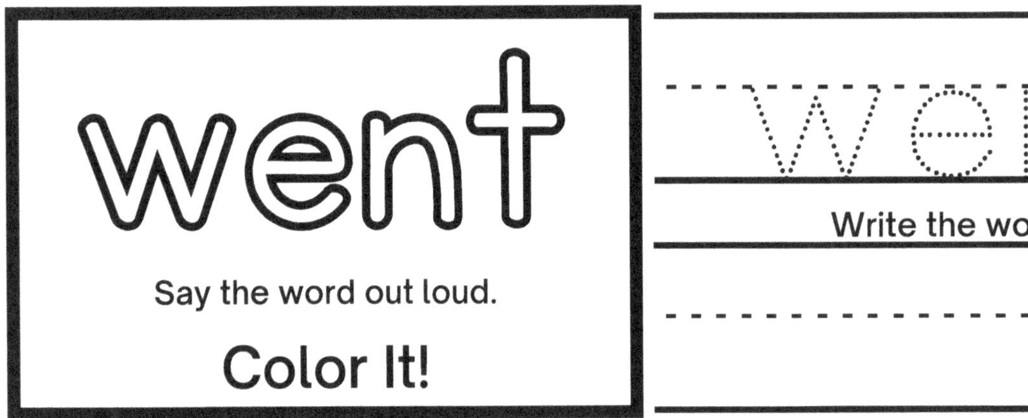

went

Say the word out loud.

Color It!

Trace the word.

went

Write the word.

Find the word in the sentence and circle it . Trace the word.

Remmi went outside.

Dad went riding on a horse.

Write the missing word.

I ____ along with the plan.

Where the bird ____ is unknown.

well

Trace the sight word:

well well well

Write the sight word:

went

Trace the sight word

went went

Write the sight word:

Sight Words

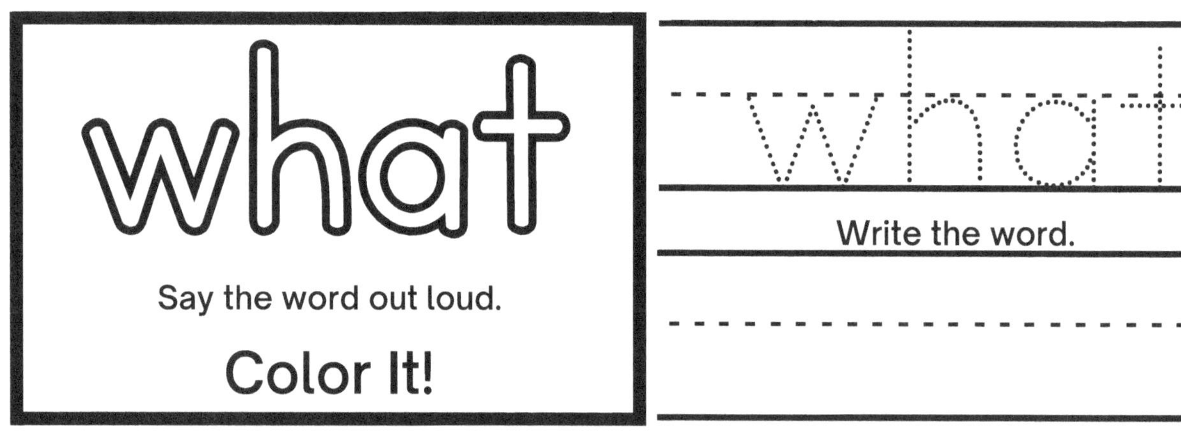

Write the word.

Find the word in the sentence and circle it . Trace the word.

I know what the boy wants.

What are you doing?

Write the missing word.

This is ____ I want to eat.

____ do you want to eat?

Draw a line to the matching **what.**

what

what

what

what

WHAT

WHAT

what

what

what

what

Find the word **what.**. It is written 4 times

a	k	d	**w**	m
o	r	**w**	**h**	a
s	**w**	**h**	**a**	**t**
w	**h**	**a**	**t**	d
p	s	**t**	i	s

Sight Words

Say the word out loud.

Color It!

Trace the word.

Write the word.

Find the word in the sentence and circle it . Trace the word.

The clouds are white.

John has a white dog.

Write the missing word.

I put on my ____ shirt.

Grandpa has _____ hair.

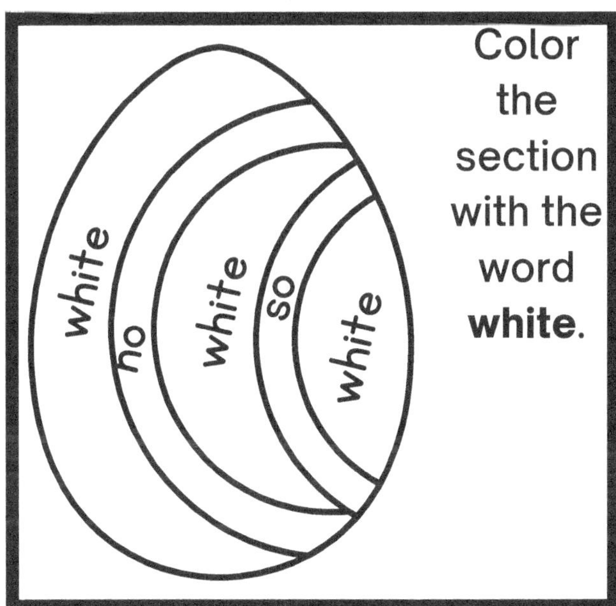

Color the section with the word **white**.

Trace the sight word:

Write the sight word:

Trace the sight word:

Write the sight word:

Sight Words

Trace the word.

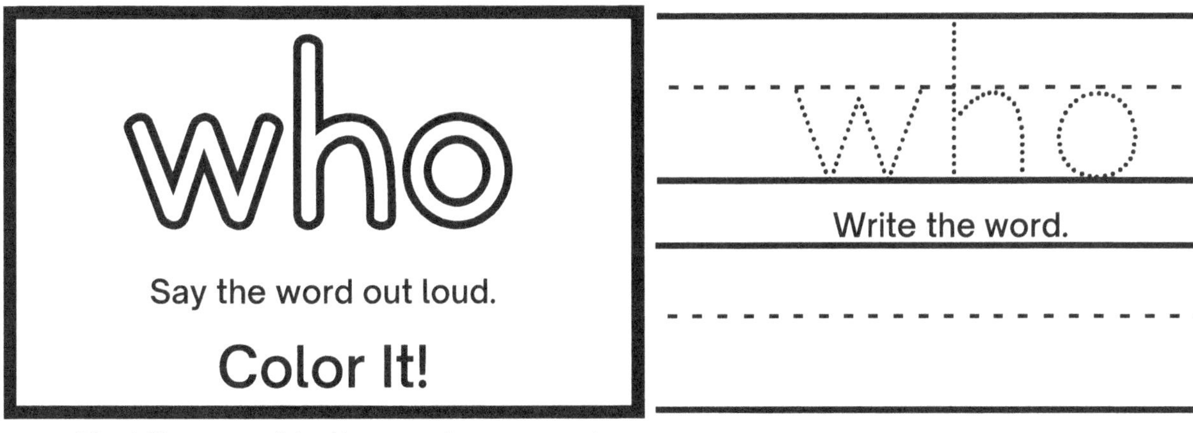

Write the word.

Find the word in the sentence and circle it . Trace the word.

Who is at the door?

John is who won the prize.

Write the missing word.

___ gave you that shirt.

Al is the person ___ gave it,.

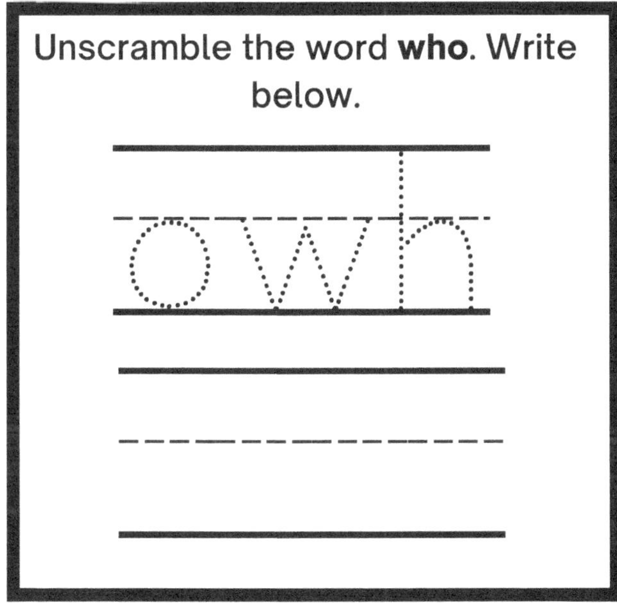

Sight Words

Say the word out loud.

Color It!

Trace the word.

Write the word.

Find the word in the sentence and circle it . Trace the word.

The store will close soon.

Will he go home on the bus?

Write the missing word.

What ____ be in the box?

Grandpa ____ call today.

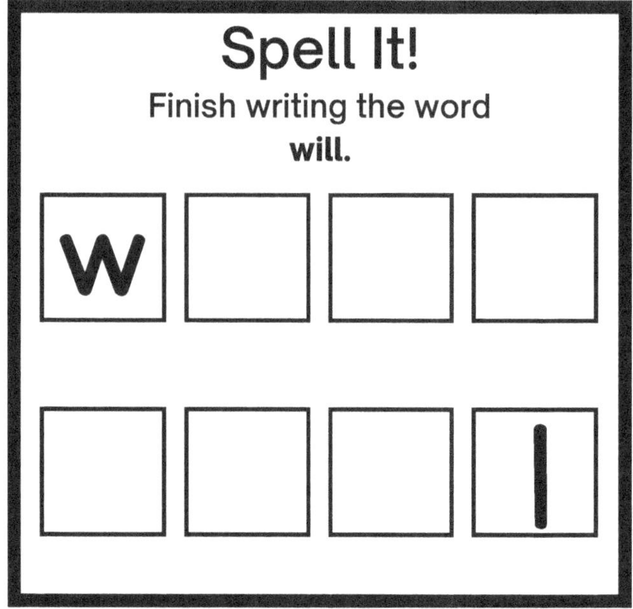

Trace the sight word:

who who who

Write the sight word:

will

Trace the sight word:

will will will

Write the sight word:

Sight Words

Say the word out loud.

Color It!

Trace the word.

Write the word.

Find the word in the sentence and circle it . Trace the word.

Mom is with my dad.

He went with me home.

Write the missing word.

What comes ____ the lunch?

Grandpa is ____ us today.

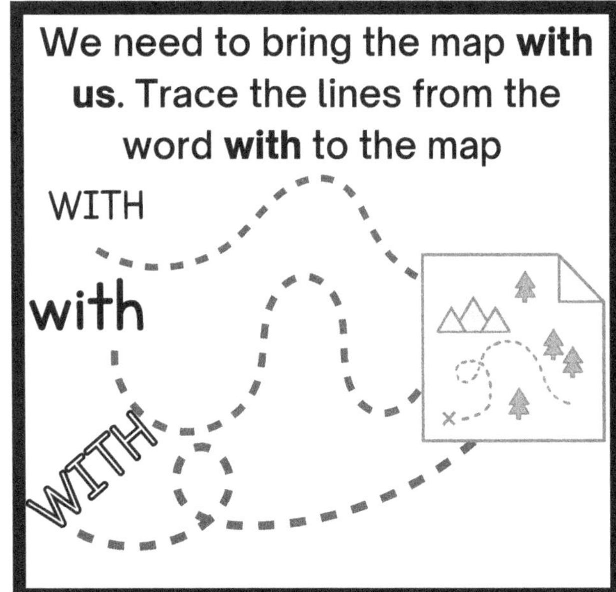

Find the word **with**. It is written 4 times

w	i	t	h	r
i	r	w	v	i
t	w	i	t	h
h	z	t	d	h
a	p	h	c	e

Sight Words

yes

Say the word out loud.

Color It!

Write the word.

Find the word in the sentence and circle it . Trace the word.

Hazel said yes to the question.

Yes ,he will go home on the bus?

Write the missing word.

Is that a ___ ?

Grandpa said ___ to coming.

Finish the word **yes** by writing the missing letter.

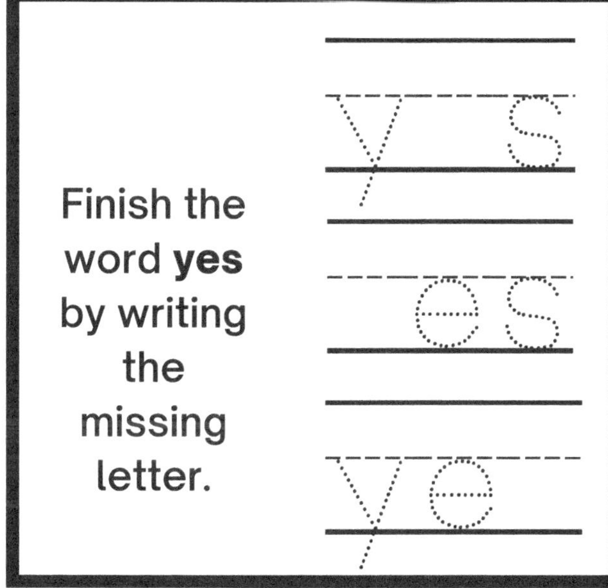

Draw a line to the matching **yes.**

yes

yes

yes

yes

YES

YES

yes

yes

yes

yes

Trace the sight word:

with with with

Write the sight word:

yes

Trace the sight word:

yes yes yes

Write the sight word:

Learning Through Repetition

<u>Directions:</u>

Each page is is filled with two sight words. Color each sight word. On the following pages, are examples of each word used in sentences. Trace the word and fill in the missing sight word. Cut out each page and each sight word and use them as flash cards. You can laminate them and use them as a flash card.

Track the process. After each page have the early learner color the designated sight word reward!

I can read

Track the learning. After each page color your reward.

Track the learning. After each page color your reward.

Track the learning. After each page color your reward.

too · under · want · was

well · went · what · white

who · will · with · yes

all

am

All of us went to the store.
I see all of the picture.

___ the cats meow for food.
I see ___ the girls.

I am at home.
Am I going to see you?

I __ hungry.
__ I ahead of you?

are

at

Find the word in the sentence and
circle it . Trace the word.

We are going home.

The dogs are running fast.

Write the missing word.

The birds ___ singing. .

What ___ you doing?

Find the word in the sentence and
circle it . Trace the word.

The plane is at the airport.

My dad is at the store.

Write the missing word.

Look __ the mirror.

The cat is __ the vet's office.

ate

be

Find the word in the sentence and
circle it . Trace the word.

I ate lunch with Nana.

I ate an apple.

Write the missing word.

The class ___ lunch together.

The dog ___ my sandwich.

Find the word in the sentence and
circle it . Trace the word.

I will be home later.

Birds can be loud.

Write the missing word.

We have to __ at school later.

When will you __ here?

black

brown

Find the word in the sentence and
circle it . Trace the word.

Zebras are black and white.
The newspaper's ink is black.

Write the missing word.

They have _____ hair.
Write in _____ ink.

Find the word in the sentence and
circle it . Trace the word.

The box is brown.
The girl has brown eyes.

Write the missing word.

The puppy has _____ fur.
My shoes are _____ .

but

came

Find the word in the sentence and circle it . Trace the word.

I tried to stop but could not.
The day is beautiful but cold.

Write the missing word.

I can't, ___ Tom can go.
I have the lock ___ not the key.

.

Find the word in the sentence and circle it . Trace the word.

He came with me to the store .
The bus came to pick us up.

Write the missing word.

The box ____ in the mail .
She ____ to eat with us.

did

do

Find the word in the sentence and
circle it . Trace the word.

Did you know the answer?
He did his homework.

Write the missing word.

That is what he ___ .
What ___ she say?

Find the word in the sentence and
circle it . Trace the word.

We should do that again.
Do not let him out.

Write the missing word.

I have to __ my homework.
Where __ they live?

eat

four

Find the word in the sentence and
circle it . Trace the word.

We should eat now.
Let her eat her food.

Write the missing word.

I have to ___ lunch still.
Where did you ___ lunch?

Find the word in the sentence and
circle it . Trace the word.

Maddie is four years old.
She got four boxes in the mail.

Write the missing word.

There are ____ cakes.

Why do you need ____ balls?

get

good

Find the word in the sentence and
circle it . Trace the word.

I am here to get the pie.
How do I get there?

Write the missing word.

___ help!
What do I ___ for you?

Find the word in the sentence and
circle it . Trace the word.

He did good on the test.
The food tasted good .

Write the missing word.

Kate was ____ at school.
Is the music ____ ?

have

he

Find the word in the sentence and
circle it . Trace the word.
I have the box.
What do you have ?
Write the missing word.
You ____ a dog
____ you tried the cake?

Find the word in the sentence and
circle it . Trace the word.
He likes turtles.
What does he want?
Write the missing word.
__ has a dog.
Has __ tried the cake?

into

like

Find the word in the sentence and
circle it . Trace the word.

Frogs jumped into the pond.
The boy went into the house.

Write the missing word.

Jack lead them ____ the bus.
He wanted ____ the house?

Find the word in the sentence and
circle it . Trace the word.

Some bugs like to bite.
They like to talk.

Write the missing word.

Jane did not ____ the cake.
Do you ____ candy?

must

new

Find the word in the sentence and
circle it . Trace the word.

Sarah must wear a hat.

Must we read the book?

Write the missing word.

You ____ read the book.

We ____ not be late.

Find the word in the sentence and
circle it . Trace the word.

I am new here.

I have a new boy in my class.

Write the missing word.

You can buy a ___ car.

Do you have a ___ cat?

no

now

Find the word in the sentence and
circle it . Trace the word.

There are no stairs.
David said no .

Write the missing word.

There is __ candy left.
Did she say __ ?

Find the word in the sentence and
circle it . Trace the word.

You are now home.
Give me the ball now .

Write the missing word.

I feel better ___ .
___ I can say I am finished?

on

our

Find the word in the sentence and
circle it . Trace the word.

He is on the swing.
I left my book on the bus.

Write the missing word.

Tillie went __ an airplane.
What is going __ ?

Find the word in the sentence and
circle it . Trace the word.

We gave our toys away.
This is our ball.

Write the missing word.

You can give ___ cake away.
Do you want ___ help?

out

please

Find the word in the sentence and
circle it . Trace the word.

They store was out of milk.
Maddie held out her hand.

Write the missing word.

You can go __ the door.
Do you want to ___ to play?

Find the word in the sentence and
circle it . Trace the word.

Please help clean up.
Follow me please.

Write the missing word.

You can do as you ______ .
______ give this to your dad?

pretty

ran

The flower is pretty.
Jane drew a pretty picture.

The bird had _______ features.
How _______ was the picture?

I ran fast.
The fox ran away.

You ___ fast .
The boy ___ up the stairs.

ride

saw

I ride the bus to school.
Allyson could ride the bike.

She can ____ the elephant.
Can you ____ the horse?

We saw the lion at the zoo.
Jason saw a movie.

She ___ him cross the finish line.
Who ___ the movie with Jason?

say

she

Find the word in the sentence and
circle it . Trace the word.
Say that again please.
I won't say anything else.
Write the missing word.
He had to ___ goodbye.
What did she ___ ?

Find the word in the sentence and
circle it . Trace the word.
She is going to school.
What did she bake?
Write the missing word.
___ went for a ride.
Did ___ want to go fishing?

so

soon

I love you so much.
Roger won so many prizes.

It wasn't __ bad.
Let's finish __ we can go?

Soon we can eat lunch.
David will be home soon .

I have to go ____ .
Do you need to go ____ ?

that

there

Find the word in the sentence and
circle it . Trace the word.

That toy is mine.

I wish that I had more time.

Write the missing word.

Did you do ____ ?

____ was fun.

Find the word in the sentence and
circle it . Trace the word.

Is there any candy left?

There is a dog in my chair.

Write the missing word.

I went _____ for a visit.

Did you know I live _____ ?

they

this

I wish they had made a pie.

They are home.

This is the school bus ____ ride.

____ like bananas.

This is my favorite food.

I can see this.

____ makes me smile.

Do you like ____ ?

too

under

Find the word in the sentence and
circle it . Trace the word.

Love you too.

It is too far to go.

Write the missing word.

It is never ___ late.

Do you want to go ___ ?

Find the word in the sentence and
circle it . Trace the word.

We sat under the tree.

I can see under the water.

Write the missing word.

_____ the tree sat three boys.

Are you _____ the tree?

want

was

We want to play outside.
I want go to the store.

I _____ him to be happy.
Do you _____ the toy?

She was looking out the window.
He was riding the bus home.

The book ___ good.
Where ___ the boy?

well

went

I hope the race went well.
He rides the bus home as well .

____ , let us go now.
Is he going as ____ ?

Remmi went outside.
Dad went riding on a horse.

I ____ along with the plan.
Where the bird ____ is unknown.

what

white

I know what the boy wants.
What are you doing?

This is ____ I want to eat.
____ do you want to eat?

The clouds are white .
John has a white dog.

I put on my ____ shirt.
Grandpa has ____ hair.

who

will

Find the word in the sentence and
circle it . Trace the word.

Who is at the door?

John is who won the prize.

Write the missing word.

___ gave you that shirt.

Al is the person ___ gave it.

Find the word in the sentence and
circle it . Trace the word.

The store will close soon.

Will he go home on the bus?

Write the missing word.

What ____ be in the box?

Grandpa ____ call today.

with

yes

Find the word in the sentence and
circle it . Trace the word.

Mom is with my dad.

He went with me home.

Write the missing word.

What comes ____ the lunch?

Grandpa is ____ us today.

Find the word in the sentence and
circle it . Trace the word.

Hazel said yes to the question.

Yes ,he will go home on the bus?

Write the missing word.

Is that a ___ ?

Grandpa said ___ to coming.